Frederick Davis Greene

The Armenian Crisis in Turkey

The massacre of 1894, its antecedents and significance, with a consideration of some of the factors which enter into the solution of this phase of the Eastern question

Frederick Davis Greene

The Armenian Crisis in Turkey
The massacre of 1894, its antecedents and significance, with a consideration of some of the factors which enter into the solution of this phase of the Eastern question

ISBN/EAN: 9783337288228

Printed in Europe, USA, Canada, Australia, Japan

Cover: Foto ©ninafisch / pixelio.de

More available books at **www.hansebooks.com**

THE ARMENIAN CRISIS IN TURKEY

THE MASSACRE OF 1894, ITS ANTECEDENTS AND SIGNIFICANCE

BY

FREDERICK DAVIS GREENE

ILLUSTRATED

KURDISH SHEIKHS.

THE ARMENIAN CRISIS IN TURKEY

THE MASSACRE OF 1894, ITS ANTECEDENTS AND SIGNIFICANCE

WITH A CONSIDERATION OF SOME OF THE FACTORS WHICH ENTER INTO THE SOLUTION OF THIS PHASE OF THE EASTERN QUESTION

BY

FREDERICK DAVIS GREENE, M.A.

FOR SEVERAL YEARS A RESIDENT
IN ARMENIA

Յուսահատելու չենք։—ԹՐԻՄԵԱՆ ՀԱՅՐԻԿ

WITH INTRODUCTION BY REV. JOSIAH STRONG, D.D.
AUTHOR OF "OUR COUNTRY," "THE NEW ERA," ETC.

G. P. PUTNAM'S SONS
NEW YORK   LONDON
27 WEST TWENTY-THIRD ST.   24 BEDFORD ST., STRAND
The Knickerbocker Press
1895

TO THE MEMORY
OF THE
VICTIMS OF THE SASSOUN MASSACRE
1894
I DEDICATE
THIS APPEAL TO THE CIVILIZED WORLD
IN BEHALF OF THEIR RACE AND OF ALL THE
RACES IN TURKEY

INTRODUCTION.

THIS is an important book. It deals with a burning question, and in a way which will command public attention and public confidence.

The author is thoroughly equipped for his task. Birth, residence, and travel in Turkey have made him personally acquainted with the situation which he discusses, and the independence of his position enables him to write without restraint and without prejudice. After nearly four years of service as a missionary of the American Board in Van, the centre of Armenia, during which no criticism of his course was ever made either by the Board or by the Turkish Government, he was recently ordered by his physician to return to America. Having resigned his connection with the American Board, he writes as the representative of no society, religious or political, and is connected with none. In issuing this book he is simply discharging what to him is a personal and unavoidable obligation; and as he frankly avows its authorship, it will be impossible for the Turkish Government to hold any one else responsible for it.

The author shows that the case of the subject races in the Ottoman Empire is desperate, that there is no hope of reform from within, and that relief must therefore come through the interference of the powers of Europe. Their action depends largely on the support of the public. "*Public opinion*," therefore, "*must be brought to bear upon this case*," as Mr. Gladstone said in the House of Commons six years ago. Since then there has been added a new chapter of horrors, and the demand for decisive action in the name of our common humanity has become more urgent. The facts furnished by this book ought to arouse such public opinion as will justify and compel prompt and efficient action on the part of the Powers.

The United States need not depart from its long-established foreign policy, but is bound to protect its own honor and the lives and property of its citizens.

JOSIAH STRONG.

NEW YORK, March 1, 1895.

CONTENTS.

CHAPTER	PAGE
I.—A CHAPTER OF HORRORS	1

Certified Evidence of the Armenian Massacre, Preceded by an Endorsement of the Evidence, with Signatures in Fac-simile, and an Explanatory Note.

II.—GENERAL INFORMATION ABOUT EASTERN TURKEY	43

The Physical Aspects, Inhabitants, and Administration of the Country.

III.—THE CHRONIC CONDITION OF ARMENIA AND KURDISTAN	54

Specific and Detailed Instances of Kurdish Plunder and Oppression.—The Turkish System of Taxation and its Abuses.—Why these Facts are so little Known.—What can be Done to Improve the Situation.

IV.—OTTOMAN PROMISES AND THEIR FULFILMENT,	70

The Treaty of Adrianople, 1829.—The Hatti Sherif, 1839.—Pledge of 1844.—Protestant Charter, 1850.—Hatti Humayoun, 1856.—Anglo-Turkish Convention, 1878.—Treaty of Berlin, 1878.

V.—THE OUTCOME OF THE TREATY OF BERLIN	76

British Naval Demonstration, 1879.—The Identical Note of the Powers, 1880, and the Turkish Reply.—The Collective Note of the Powers, and the Aggressive Response of the Sublime Porte.—The Circular of Great Britain, 1881, its Cool Reception by the Powers, and the Indefinite Postponement of Turkish Reforms.—The Effect of the Berlin Treaty in Arousing Armenian Aspirations and Increasing Turkish Oppression.—Armenian Revolution a Nightmare of the Turks.—The

CHAPTER		PAGE
	Real Armenian Position.—The Only Treatment for the "Sick Man" a Surgical One.	
VI.—	THE SULTAN AND THE SUBLIME PORTE	87
	The Demands of his Office as Sultan-Calif.—Justice to Christian and Moslem both Impossible.—Status of non-Mohammedans.—The Palace and the Porte.—A House Divided against Itself.	
VII.—	PREVIOUS ACTS OF THE TURKISH TRAGEDY,	95
	The Massacres of Greeks, 1822; Nestorians, 1850; Syrians, 1860; Cretans, 1867; Bulgarians, 1876; Yezidis, 1892; Armenians, 1894.	
VIII.—	ISLAM AS A FACTOR OF THE PROBLEM	110
	A Politico-Religious System.—Indissoluble and Incapable of Modification.—The Military, Civil, and Legal Rights of non-Mohammedans.—Freeman's Conclusion.	
IX.—	GLADSTONE ON THE ARMENIAN MASSACRE AND ON TURKISH MISRULE	121
X.—	WHO ARE THE ARMENIANS?	131
	Their Origin, History, Church, Language, Literature, and General Characteristics.	
XI.—	AMERICANS IN TURKEY, THEIR WORK AND INFLUENCE	147
	Their Attitude and Recognized Position.—Statistics of the Direct Results of their Efforts.—Their Indirect Influence on All Classes.—The Present Threatening Attitude of the Turkish Government.	
Appendix A.—	A BIT OF AMERICAN DIPLOMACY	157
B.—	ESTABLISHMENT OF U. S. CONSULATES IN EASTERN TURKEY	163
C.—	DR. CYRUS HAMLIN'S EXPLANATION	167
D.—	THE CENSORSHIP OF THE PRESS	169
E.—	BIBLIOGRAPHY OF THE SUBJECT	171
GENERAL INDEX		175

LIST OF ILLUSTRATIONS.

	PAGE
KURDISH SHEIKHS	*Frontispiece*
FAC-SIMILE OF SIGNATURES	2 and 4
VICTIMS OF TURKISH TAXATION	10
REVIEW OF KURDISH CAVALRY	19
NAREG: ANCIENT CHURCH AND MODERN HOVELS	29
ARMENIAN GIRLS OF VAN	39
A KURD OF THE OLD TYPE	47
RUINED KURDISH CASTLE AT KHOSHAB	50
MINAS TCHÉRAZ	80
ZEIBEK "IRREGULAR"	83
TURKISH SOLDIER, "REGULAR"	85
H. I. M. SULTAN ABD-UL-HAMID KHAN	91
HIGHWAY IN ARMENIA	105
ARMENIAN REBELS WHO WOULD NOT PAY TAXES	120
KURDISH HAMIDIÉH SOLDIERS, EXECUTING THE "SWORD-DANCE"	127
ANCIENT ARMENIAN TOMBSTONE	135
THE CATHOLICOS OF ETCHMIADZIN	139
THE SUBORDINATE CATHOLICOS OF AGHTAMAR	141
THE ISLAND MONASTERY OF AGHTAMAR	145
ARMENIAN FAMILY OF BITLIS	152

PREFACE.

THE writer has, from his birth, been a student of the Eastern Question, but makes no claim to having mastered it. What he has learned of the phases of that question here treated has been by absorption, observation, travel, residence, and investigation, in the land itself, and by study and reading in regard to it. The very short time allowed in the preparation of this humble contribution to the subject has necessitated a hasty and partial treatment at the expense of literary form. Some of the material of the second and third chapters and most of the illustrations in this book are reproduced from an article by the author in the American *Review of Reviews* for January, 1895, by the kind permission of the editor, Dr. Albert Shaw. No pains have been spared to insure accuracy. References to authorities have been given as far as possible, but in regard to much information from most reliable sources names must be withheld. It is a very significant feature of the situation in Turkey, that people who are thousands of miles away from her, and who may never set foot there again, do not dare to publicly state the facts, lest vengeance may be taken on their families and friends, still within reach of Turkish violence and intrigue. If His Imperial Majesty, the Sultan, but knew the real facts of the atrocious massacre of last year, and realized the disgrace attaching to the Turkish name on account of the unspeakably brutal deeds of his Turkish and Kurdish soldiers, officers included, we cannot but hope that some punishment would be visited upon them, experience to the contrary. He certainly should welcome the revelations of this book, and do all in his power to protect any who may aid him in bringing the facts to light and securing a better state of affairs. God help him, and save all his subjects, Turk, Arab, and Kurd, Christian, Jew, and Pagan, from the curse of a system of government not only " sick," but dead and rotting!

I preach no crusade; none is needed. But it is high time for the conscience of Europe and America to assert itself not simply the " non-Conformist conscience," but the Established, the Orthodox, the Catholic, the Agnostic, and the Infidel conscience, in fact the human conscience—against this crime upon humanity. If this conscience is once aroused, I care not what parties are in power, or how the game stands on the diplomatic chessboard, the Eastern Question will be settled, instead of forever threatening the peace of Europe, and one more blot will be wiped out from the annals of the world.

I use the title THE CRISIS IN TURKEY because there *is* a crisis in the history of one of her most important races; there *ought* to be one throughout Turkey; and there *may* be one in Europe if selfishness, jealousy, and duplicity are forever to stifle all considerations of humanity, national honor, and—I blush to add it—of Christianity.

In order to protect "British interests," for two-score years, not to say longer, has "Christian" England stood guard at the Sublime Porte, warning all intruders away. With her hand on the door of the Turk's disorderly house, she has complacently informed the world that she in particular—as well as the other Powers—has secured promises, and even guaranties, that all would go well. But all the while, Her Majesty's Ministers, of whatever party, have heard the bitter and despairing cry of the poor wretches within. These Ministers have, since 1881, with rare exceptions, carefully suppressed in their archives the consular reports which have officially kept them informed of the real state of affairs.[1] And all the while, England's share of the profits of this partnership with the unspeakable Turk has been steadily dropping into her overflowing coffers. Was Cyprus nothing? Is the interest on Turkish bonds nothing? Of course the creditor

---

[1] "I am at a loss to know why the Reports of Consuls ceased to be furnished in or about the year 1881. Consuls are supposed to keep their eyes open and to report facts regarding the people among whom they live, and it is altogether a new idea that their Reports are to be regarded as confidential documents. If they are to be so, that is simply condemning the Consuls' Reports to perpetual barrenness and absolute inutility. Why are not consular reports to be made, and being made, why are they not to be printed? If in this respect I am personally, or anyone associated with me, is open to censure, let the facts be brought out; but do not let a particular act at a particular time be confounded with the adoption of the principle of eternal silence about the horrors that prevail in Armenia."—Speech by the Rt. Hon. W. E. Gladstone, in House of Commons, May 28, 1889.

must have his due, even though it is extracted in blood-drops by a pressure that England and the other Powers help to maintain.

A famous London divine recently preached a sermon in connection with the Armenian Massacre, using as a text Ezra ix., 3: "And when I heard this thing, I rent my garment and my mantle, and plucked off the hair of my head and of my beard, and sat down astonied." May I suggest that it is high time to rouse oneself from mere astonishment, as did the Hebrew prophet? If the eloquent preacher is at a loss for an appropriate text for another sermon to an English audience, he can find it in the sixth verse of the same chapter: "O my God, I am ashamed and blush to lift up my face to thee, my God: for our iniquities are increased over our head, and our trespass is grown up unto the heavens."

The very well informed correspondent of *The Speaker* wrote from Constantinople two months ago: "I fear there can be no doubt about the essential facts. We have already the official reports of the consuls at Van, Erzeroom, Sivas, and Diarbekir, which have not yet been published, but which, we know, confirm the most horrible statements made in the newspapers. We have the reports of the Armenian refugees who were eye-witnesses. We have the reports sent to the Armenian Patriarchate here, and the reports of Catholic and Protestant missionaries in the vicinity of Sasun. Beyond this, and most horrible of all, we have the testimony of the Turkish soldiers who took part in the massacres. These soldiers have talked with the greatest freedom in public places, and to all who would listen, boasting of their deeds. We have full reports from all these places of the statements made by hundreds of these soldiers, and they agree in all essential points."[1]

The author does not ignore the repeated and earnest efforts that have been made for years, by such individual Englishmen as the Hon. James Bryce, to call attention to the condition of Armenia. Their protests have kept alive Armenian hope that England at least would not entirely repudiate her obligations. But the futility of these same protests has also given assurance to the Sublime Porte in carrying out its policy of repression and extermination in Armenia.

Of course neither the party in power, nor its successors, will proceed energetically unless assured of the support of the people whom they represent. As soon as there is sufficient pressure from behind something more will be done than to dally with Turkish Commissions of Inquiry, sent under circumstances which make a true and full report simply a physical and moral impossibility.[2] The Turk is on trial and should be allowed to plead "Not Guilty." But it is not customary, in courts where justice is the object, to allow the criminal at the bar the privilege of act-

[1] *The Speaker*, London, January 12, 1895.

[2] "A good deal of misapprehension exists with respect to the constitution of the Commission of Inquiry. It is not an international but a Turkish Commission, and, to judge by past experience, Turkish Commissions are instruments by which truth is suppressed and issues are obscured. It is satisfactory that representatives of Great Britain, France, and Russia will have the opportunity of examining the *procès-verbaux*, besides being present at the sittings of the Commission; and

ing also as the prosecuting attorney, and of summoning and examining the witnesses. As is well known, the most stringent measures have been taken by the Sublime Porte to prevent any representative of the press from watching the proceedings of the Commission of Inquiry at Moosh, or from making any independent investigation on the ground. Such precautions are hardly necessary, for all evidence of the massacre was concealed by torch and spade six months ago. If the executioners themselves overlooked any of their victims, the jackals, dogs, and vultures have surely found them by this time.

There are fifty native-born American citizens, not counting their children, who are now buried in Eastern Turkey. The fanatical outbreak which has slain thousands in their midst may yet involve them. The President of the United States long ago ordered a U. S. Consul to make a report as to the facts, simply for his own government, which has no official knowledge of what has or is taking place in that isolated region. The Sultan stamped his foot, and Consul Jewett was told to put his instructions in his pocket, where they still remain.[1]

As for France, who tattoos her fair figure with " *Liberté, Égalité, Fraternité* " wherever there is

credit is due to the British Foreign Office for having taken the initiative in securing this concession ; but it must be remembered that the powers of the international representatives will be strictly limited, and that they will not be able to guarantee the security of the witnesses."
— F. S. Stevenson, M.P., "Armenia," in *The Contemporary Review*, February, 1895.

[1] See APPENDIX B on the establishment of new U. S. Consulates in Eastern Turkey. Also APPENDIX A on American Diplomacy.

space to write the words, she evidently confines her motto to herself. It is reported that at the close of the Berlin Treaty of 1878, Prince Bismarck expressed his sentiments by saying that he "would not give one Pomeranian grenadier for the Balkan Peninsula." If so, probably he would sacrifice even less now for Armenia. Have the German people nothing to say?

Holy Russia feels so sure of the Armenian apple, which seems bound to fall into her lap, that she does n't even care to shake the branch, unmindful of the fact that the apple is tenacious of its hold, and is being pecked to pieces and rotting on the stem. Austria would not refuse the task of instituting reforms as far south as Salonica. Poor Italy is willing to be useful, and Greece does not care to be left out. They all want their share. Nobody expects or is trying to secure reforms from within, though promises to that effect may still be demanded, and will always be ready on demand.

As for official Turkey, she has long seen the sword of Damocles over her head, and will bow to the stroke of Fate whenever it falls. If it only comes hard enough, and is aimed true to the mark, she will even get out of the way. *Not a drop of blood need be shed.*

What is the real difficulty in Turkey? Is it a conflict of race or religion? *Primarily* it is neither, though both these elements complicate the case. *In one word it is misgovernment.* Do not be deceived by this rather mild word, and dismiss the subject with the reflection that "there is misgovernment everywhere." Misgovernment as it exists in Turkey is an organization that breeds death and corruption.

It is a disease, of which the germs penetrate the whole system of the body politic. It is a disease, hereditary, chronic, and fastened upon the very vitals of its victim. No creed is exempt, every race is attacked by it. The more apparent result is outward impoverishment and material prostration. The more dangerous and deplorable symptom is the moral deterioration of all the races affected.

I am no eulogist of the mass of Armenians in their present condition. But I know their grand possibilities as a race, physically, intellectually, and morally. The depths to which an individual or a race can fall indicate the height which might have been attained. The only wonder is that a people of so great ability, energy, and spirit have so long submitted. But when one sees, as I have been compelled to, during years of residence both in Constantinople and the interior, how the fetters have been forged on every limb, and how the movement of a finger even brings down immediate and terrible vengeance, the wonder arises why these wretches are so foolhardy as to undertake revolution. The fact is they are not engaged in any such enterprise. Individual agitators there are, but even their object is only to force the civilized world to give attention to the despairing cry of their race, which even God does not seem, to them, to hear.

The case of the Armenians demands immediate and thorough attention. But the Armenian question should not be allowed to fill the whole horizon in the Levant. Just now the blaze comes from their house, but no one can tell when it may result in a general conflagration. All the other Christian races and the Mohammedan races, too, are equally concerned. Europe itself is endangered, as her statesmen well know, and safety depends only on their prompt and united action.

I have seen the crushing and—what is worse—demoralizing conditions from which the Armenian and all other races in Turkey suffer under Moslem misrule. I know how rapidly these fine races would advance along every line, were these conditions changed. It is my firm belief that such changes may now be secured, if the interest already aroused throughout the civilized world be expressed in intelligent and determined action. In the hope of such action I send forth this little book. If action is *not* taken, the effect of this book, as of all agitation in behalf of the victims of Turkey, will be to draw the fetters deeper. What result may follow to my many friends and former associates on the ground, with whom it is very difficult to communicate, I do not know. But I know them, and do not believe that there is one among their number who, to shield himself from danger, would stay my pen.

Reader, your voice and help are needed.

" He 's true to God who 's true to man ; wherever wrong is done
To the humblest and the weakest, 'neath the all-beholding sun,
That wrong is also done to us ; and they are slaves most base
Whose love of right is for themselves, and not for all their race."
—LOWELL.

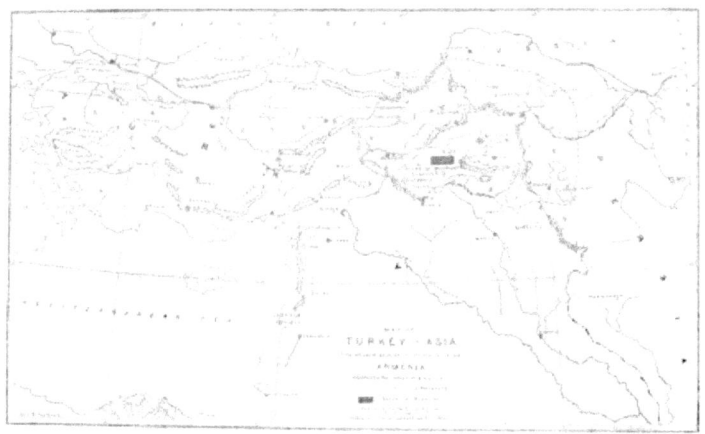

CHAPTER I.

A CHAPTER OF HORRORS.

CERTIFIED EVIDENCE OF THE MASSACRE IN SASSOUN.

WE, the undersigned, by examination and comparison, have satisfied ourselves that the following statements are verbatim reports, written under the dates which they bear, by American citizens who have spent from six to thirty years in Eastern Turkey. We have examined also the fact that they are written from six different cities from one hundred to two hundred miles apart, but forming a circle about the centre in which the massacres occurred. For the personal safety of the writers the names of the places cannot now be made public. They are independent reports from a country where refugees and returned soldiers of the Sultan speak of what they know. We have the utmost confidence in these statements and regard them worthy the belief of all men.

In the name of a suffering humanity we urge the careful perusal of these statements, and recommend that all readers take measures to make the indignation of an outraged Christian world effectually felt. We deprecate revolution among these helpless Turkish subjects, but bespeak cordial co-operation in bringing to bear upon Turkey the force of the righteous condemnation of our seventy millions of people.

Frederic T. Greenhalge

Frances E. Willard

Wm. Lloyd Garrison.

Samuel J. Barrows.

Geo. C. Lorimer

William E. Barton

H. M. Jewett

Mary A. Livermore

Alpheus H. Hardy

Francis E. Clark.

FREDERIC T. GREENHALGE
> Governor of Massachusetts.

FRANCES E. WILLARD
> President National W. C. T. U.

WM. LLOYD GARRISON

SAMUEL J. BARROWS
> Editor *Christian Register*.

GEO. C. LORIMER
> Pastor Tremont Temple, Boston.

WILLIAM E. BARTON
> Pastor Shawmut Church, Boston.

H. M. JEWETT
> Ex-U. S. Consul, Sivas, Turkey.[1]

MARY A. LIVERMORE
> Author and Lecturer.

ALPHEUS H. HARDY

FRANCIS E. CLARK
> Pres. United Society Christian Endeavor.

[1] Brother and predecessor of the present Consul Jewett, at Sivas.

Julia Ward Howe.

Mancius A. Walker

S. E. Pillsbury.

Isabel Somerset

Cyrus Hamlin

J. J. Lansing

Joseph Cook

R. R. Russell

Jonathan A. Lane

EDWARD EVERETT HALE
Pastor New South Congregational Church, Boston.

JULIA WARD HOWE
Author and Lecturer.

FRANCIS A. WALKER
Pres. Mass. School of Technology.

A. E. PILLSBURY
Ex-Attorney-General of Massachusetts.

ISABEL SOMERSET
Lady Henry Somerset.

CYRUS HAMLIN
Founder of Robert College.

I. J. LANSING
Pastor Park Street Church, Boston.

JOSEPH COOK
Author and Lecturer.

WM. E. RUSSELL
Ex-Governor of Massachusetts.

JONATHAN A. LANE
Pres. Boston Merchants' Association.

EXPLANATORY NOTE BY THE AUTHOR.

THESE letters are written by men who can have no possible motive for misrepresenting the facts in the case, while, on the other hand, each writer subjected himself to personal danger by putting such statements upon paper and sending them through the mails. Several of the documents have gotten through Turkey by circuitous routes, in some instances having been sent by special messenger to Persia, and so on to this country. Others were never risked in the Turkish mails, but have come through the British post-office at Constantinople.

It must be borne in mind that no writer was an eye-witness of the actual massacre; nor could he have been, inasmuch as the whole region was surrounded by a military cordon during the massacre and for months after. The letters are largely based on the testimony of refugees from that region, or of Kurds and soldiers who participated in the butchery, and who had no hesitation in speaking about the affair in public or private until long after, when the prospect of a European investigation sealed their lips. Much of the evidence is, therefore, essentially first hand, having been obtained from eye-witnesses, by parties in the vicinity at the time, who are impartial, thoroughly experienced in sifting Oriental testimony, familiar with the Turkish and Armenian languages, and of the highest veracity. No one letter would have much force if taken alone, for it might be a large report of a small matter; but these sixteen letters are written independently of one another, at different times, and from seven different cities widely apart, five of them forming a circle around the scene of destruction. The evidence is cumulative and overwhelming.

There is absolute unanimity to this extent: that a gigantic and indescribably horrible massacre of Armenian men, women, and children did actually take place in the Sassoun and neighboring regions about Sept. 1, 1894, and that, too, at the hands of Kurdish troops armed by the Sultan of Turkey, as well as of regular soldiers sent under orders from the same source. What those orders were will probably never transpire. That they were executed under the personal direction of high Turkish military officers is clear. There can also be no doubt—for the official notice from the palace was printed in the Constantinople papers in November last—that Zekki Pasha, Commander of the Fourth Army Corps, who led the regular troops in the work of extermination, has since been specially honored by a decoration from the Sultan, who was also pleased to send silk banners to the four leading Kurdish chiefs, by a special messenger.

The latest, most accurate, and comprehensive document in this correspondence is No. 6, which is based on evidence obtained with special care at the nearest attainable point to the scene, and was prepared by parties in intimate relations with the European official who made the first investigation on the ground last October, but whose report has not yet been made public.

The letters are arranged in chronological order. In view of the fact that the names of the cities from which the various documents are dated must be withheld at present, these places are designated by letters of the alphabet. The separate extracts are also numbered to facilitate reference. In order that there may be no confusion, all explanatory comments of the author are enclosed in brackets.

THE EVIDENCE.

No. 1.

[The reader should take notice that this first letter was written over four months before the massacre actually occurred.]

D . . .. April 3, 1894.

It does seem in this region as if the government were bent on reducing all those who survive the process to a grovelling poverty, when they can think of nothing more than getting their daily bread. There is good reason for thinking that unless so-called Christian nations extend a helping hand, they [the Armenians] will become wellnigh extinct. Of course I do not sympathize in any way with the extremists in other lands who are stirring things up here. Nor do I agree with those papers that decry this movement as very foolish because there is no hope for success. If I rightly interpret the movement in this region, the thought is not revolution at all, but a desperate effort to call the attention of Europe to the wrongs they are suffering and will ever continue to suffer under this government. They feel that they will never succeed in attracting that attention unless they show that they are desperate enough to sacrifice their lives. *And there is no computing the lives that are going, not in open massacre as in Bulgaria—the government knows better than that,—but in secret, silent, secluded ways.* The sooner it is known, the better. There never will be peaceful, prosperous conditions here until others take hold with a strong hand.

VICTIMS OF TURKISH TAXATION ABANDONING THEIR VILLAGE HOMES.

No. 2.

[This is the first report of the massacre.]

D . . ., Sept. 26, 1894.

Troops have been massed in the region of the large plain near us. Sickness broke out among them, which took off two or three victims every few days. It was a good excuse for establishing the quarantine around, with its income from bribes, charges, and the inevitable rise in the price of the already dear grain. I suspect that one reason for placing quarantine was to hinder the information as to what all those troops were about in that region. There seems little doubt that there has been repeated in the region back of Moosh what took place in 1876 in Bulgaria. The sickening details are beginning to come in. As in that case, it has been the innocent who have been the greatest sufferers. Forty-eight villages are said to have been wholly blotted out.

No. 3.

[Efforts to conceal the truth as soon as Vice-Consul Hallward arrived on the scene, and to ward off investigation.]

D . . ., Oct. 3, 1894.

As the time goes on the extent of the slaughter seems to be confirmed as greater than was first supposed. Six thousand is a low figure—it is probably nearer ten. Mr. Hallward, the new [English] Consul at Van, has gone directly there, and it is said that the other consuls from Erzroom have also been sent to investigate. The government tried to get the people here to sign an address to the Sovereign, expressing satisfaction with his rule, disclaiming sympathy with the Armenians who have " stirred matters up," stating that the thousands slain in Talvoreeg met their just deserts, and that the four outsiders captured should be summarily punished, expressing regret that it has been thought best to send consuls to investigate, and stating that there was no need for their coming. From this document we at least get some facts that before were suppositions. It consisted of about two thousand words, and it was expected that it would be sent by telegraph with at least a thousand signatures. The Armenians here have not yet signed it, though in four districts similar papers have been secured properly sealed. *The effect of such papers on foreigners will be much modified when they know the means used to procure them.* Sword, famine, pestilence, all at once—pity this poor country!

No. 4.

[The following is from a different source.]

A . . ., Oct. 31, 1894.

We have word from Bitlis that the destruction of life in Sassoun, south of Moosh, was even greater than was supposed. The brief note which has reached us says: "Twenty-seven villages annihilated in Sassoun. Six thousand men, women, and children massacred by troops and Kourds. This awful story is just beginning to be known here, though the massacre took place early in September. The Turks have used infinite pains to prevent news leaking out, even going to the length of sending back from Trebizond many hundreds from the Moosh region who had come this way on business." This massacre was ordered from Constantinople in the sense that some Kourds having robbed Armenian villages of flocks, the Armenians pursued and tried to recover their property, and a fight ensued in which a dozen Kourds were killed. The slain were "semi-official robbers," *i. e.*, enrolled as troops and armed as such, but not under control. The authorities then telegraphed to Constantinople that Armenians had "killed some of the Sultan's troops." The Sultan at once ordered infantry and cavalry to put down the Armenian rebellion, and they did it; only, not finding any rebellion, they cleared the country so that none should occur in the future.

No. 5.

[This from a third place.]

B . . ., Nov. 16, 1894.

Last year the Talvoreeg Armenians successfully resisted the attacks of the neighboring Kourds. The country became very unsettled. This year the government interfered and sent detachments of regular soldiers to put down the Armenians. These were assisted by the Kourdish *Hamedichs* [organized troops]. The Armenians were attacked in their mountain fastnesses and were finally reduced by the failure of supplies, both of food and ammunition. About a score of villages were wiped out of existence —people slaughtered and houses burned.

A number of able-bodied young Armenians were captured, bound, covered with brushwood and burned alive. A number of Armenians, variously estimated, but less than a hundred, surrendered themselves and pled for mercy. Many of them were shot down on the spot and the remainder were dispatched with sword and bayonet.

A lot of women, variously estimated from 60 to 160 in number, were shut up in a church, and the soldiers were "let loose" among them. Many of them were outraged to death and the remainder dispatched with sword and bayonet. A lot of young women were collected as spoils of war. Two stories are told. 1. That they were carried off to the harems of their Moslem captors. 2. That they were offered Islam and the harems of their Moslem captors,—refusing, they were slaughtered. Children were placed in a row, one behind another, and a bullet fired down the line, apparently to see how many could be dispatched with one bullet. Infants and small children were piled one on the other and their heads struck off. Houses were surrounded by soldiers, set on fire, and the inmates forced back into the flames at the point of the bayonet as they tried to escape.

But this is enough of the carnage of death. Estimates vary from 3000 to 8000 for the number of persons massacred. These are sober estimates. Wild estimates place the number as high as 20,000 to 25,000.

This all took place during the latter part of August and [early part of] September. The arrival of the commander-in-chief of the Fourth Army Corps put a stop to the carnage. It is to be noted that the massacres were perpetrated by regular soldiers, for the most part under command of officers of high rank. This gives this affair a most serious aspect.

A Christian does not enjoy the respect accorded to street dogs. If this massacre passes without notice it will simply become the declaration of the doom of the Christians. There will be no security for the life, property, or honor of a Christian. A week ago last Tuesday evening at sundown a Turk kidnapped the wife of a wealthy Armenian merchant of the town of Khanoos Pert. Next morning her cries were overheard by searchers and she was rescued from a Turkish house. No redress is possible.

Wild rumors have been abroad for a long time, but trustworthy information came to hand slowly. Everything has been done to hush it all up. Some of the minor details of the stories I have told above may not be exact, but I feel quite certain they are in the main. However, that a cruelly barbarous and extensive massacre of Christians by regular soldiers assisted by Kourdish *Hamediéhs*, under command of officers of rank and responsibility, has occurred cannot be denied.

What now will the Christian world do?

No. 6.

[This is the most complete account, compiled on the ground. The following document was carefully prepared in common by parties, the signature of any one of whom would be of sufficient guaranty to give great weight. One of the party, who is largely responsible for the data given, is a man of high position and wide influence. The material was collected with the greatest difficulty and under the constant espionage of Turkish officials. Armenian Christians who were known to appear at the place where the writer was staying, were arrested and some are yet in prison if they have not met a worse fate already. The documents were sent by secret, special carriers into Persia and came by Persian post to the United States. They left Turkey about the last of November, 1894. This document alone is sufficient to stir the indignation of a Christian world.]

C . . ., Nov., 1894.

There is uneasiness in Bitlis as to the safety of that city. Scrutiny of the mails by the Turkish authorities continues, and some letters addressed to residents and officials in the United States are failing to arrive.

The *Hamedïeh* soldiers, who are Kourds, and who have been enrolled during the past three years, are uniformed to some extent, but left in their homes. They are committing all kinds of depredations. The government continues to exact taxes in the plundered districts, sends *zabtiehs*, or Turkish soldiers, to abide in the villages, and eat the people out of provisions until in some way they manage to secure the money. In the Bashkalla region many of the men find, on returning, that the government has taken possession of their property and refuses to restore it or allow them to remain in their old homes.

The authorities have taken and are taking every precaution to prevent accounts of the famous massacre of Moosh from reaching the outside world. The English consul, Mr. Hallward, went on a tour in the region affected. He was subjected to constant annoying espionage, and was absolutely unable to penetrate into the devastated region.

To what extent Armenian agitation has provoked the terrible massacre it is difficult to determine. For a year or more there seems to have been an Armenian from Constantinople staying in the region as an agitator. For a long time he skilfully evaded his pursuers, but was at last caught and taken to Bitlis. He demanded to be taken to Constantinople and to the Sultan, and, it is said, he is now living at the capital, receiving a large salary from the government. Evidently he has turned state's evidence.

FACTS REGARDING A MASSACRE AT SASSOUN, NEAR MOOSH, TURKEY.

Late in May, 1893, an outside agitator named Damatian was captured near Moosh. The government had suspected that the Talvoreeg villages were harboring such agitators, and had sent orders to certain Kourdish chiefs to attack the district, assuming the responsibility for all they should kill, and promising the Kourds all the spoil.

Not long after Damatian had been brought to Bitlis, the first week in June, the Bakranlee Kourds began to gather below Talvoreeg. As the villagers saw the Kourds gathering day by day, to the number of several thousands, they suspected their designs, and began to make preparations. On the eighth day the battle was joined. The stronger position of the villagers enabled them to do considerable execution with little loss to themselves.

The issue of the contest at sunset was some one hundred Kourds slain, and but six of the villagers, one of whom was a woman who was trying to rescue a mule from the Kourds. The villagers had succeeded in breaking down a bridge across the deep gorge of a river before a detachment of Kourds from another direction could join in the attack against them. The Kourds thus felt themselves worsted, and could not be induced to make another attack that summer.

At this juncture the Governor-general set out with troops and two field-pieces for Moosh, and infested the region near Talvoreeg, but either he considered his forces insufficient, or he had orders to keep quiet, for he made no attack, but merely had the troops keep siege. Before leaving, he succeeded, by giving hostages, in having an interview with some of the chief men in Talvoreeg, and asked them why they did not submit to the government, and pay taxes. They replied that they were not disloyal to the government, but that they could not pay taxes twice, to the Kourds and to the government. If the government would protect them, they would pay to it. Nothing came of the parley, and the siege was continued till snow fell. During the winter, while blackmail was rife in the vilayet, several rich men of Talvoreeg were invited to visit the Governor-General, but did not see best to accept.

In the early spring the Kourds of several tribes were ordered to attack the villages of Sassoun, while troops were sent on from Moosh and Bitlis, the latter taking along ammunition and stores, and ten mule-

REVIEW OF KURDISH CAVALRY BY THE GOVERNOR OF VAN, TAHIR PASHA—AT THE LEFT.

loads of kerosene (eighty cans). The whole district was pretty well besieged by Kourds and troops. The villages thus besieged would occasionally make sorties to secure food.

The Kourds on one occasion stole several oxen, and their owners tracked their property to the Kourdish tents, and found that one ox had been butchered. They asked for the others, and were refused, whereupon the villagers left, and later returned with some companions. A scrimmage ensued, in which two or three were killed on either side. The Kourds at once took their dead to the government at Moosh, and reported that the region was filled with Armenian and foreign soldiers. The government at once sent in all directions for soldiers, gathering in all from eight to ten *taboors* (regiments). Kourds congregated to the number of about twenty thousand, while some five hundred *Hamedieh* horsemen were brought to Moosh.

METHODS OF PROCEDURE AND INCIDENTS OF THE MASSACRE.

At first the Kourds were set on, and the troops kept out of sight. The villagers, put to the fight, and thinking they had only the Kourds to do with, repulsed them on several occasions. The Kourds were unwilling to do more unless the troops assisted. Some of the troops assumed Kourdish dress, and helped them in the fight with more success. Small companies of troops entered several villages, saying they had come to protect them as loyal subjects, and were quartered among the houses.

In the night they arose and slew the sleeping villagers, man, woman, and child.

By this time those in other villages were beginning to feel that extermination was the object of the government, and desperately determined to sell their lives as dearly as possible. And then began a campaign of butchery that lasted some twenty-three days, or, roughly, from the middle of August to the middle of September. The *Ferik* Pasha [Marshal Zekki Pasha], who came post-haste from Erzingan, read the Sultan's firman for extermination, and then, hanging the document on his breast, exhorted the soldiers not to be found wanting in their duty. *On the last day of August, the anniversary of the Sultan's accession, the soldiers were especially urged to distinguish themselves, and they made it the day of the greatest slaughter.* Another marked day occurred a few days earlier, being marked by the occurrence of a wonderful meteor.

No distinctions were made between persons or villages, as to whether they were loyal and had paid their taxes or not. The orders were to make a clean sweep. A priest and some leading men from one village went out to meet an officer, taking in their hands their tax receipts, declaring their loyalty, and begging for mercy; but the village was surrounded, and all human beings put to the bayonet. A large and strong man, the chief of one village, was captured by the Kourds, who tied him, threw him on the ground, and, squatting around him, stabbed him to pieces.

At Galogozan many young men were tied hand

and foot, laid in a row, covered with brushwood and burned alive. Others were seized and hacked to death piecemeal. At another village a priest and several leading men were captured, and promised release if they would tell where others had fled, but, after telling, all but the priest were killed. A chain was put around the priest's neck, and pulled from opposite sides till he was several times choked and revived, after which several bayonets were planted upright, and he raised in the air and let fall upon them.

The men of one village, when fleeing, took the women and children, some five hundred in number, and placed them in a sort of grotto in a ravine. After several days the soldiers found them, and butchered those who had not died of hunger.

Sixty young women and girls were selected from one village and placed in a church, when the soldiers were ordered to do with them as they liked, after which they were butchered.

In another village fifty choice women were set aside and urged to change their faith and become *hanums* in Turkish harems, but they indignantly refused to deny Christ, preferring the fate of their fathers and husbands. People were crowded into houses which were then set on fire. In one instance a little boy ran out of the flames, but was caught on a bayonet and thrown back.

Children were frequently held up by the hair and cut in two, or had their jaws torn apart. Women with child were ripped open; older children were pulled apart by their legs. A handsome, newly wedded couple fled to a hilltop; soldiers followed, and told them they were pretty and would be spared if they would accept Islam, but the thought of the horrible death they knew would follow did not prevent them from confessing Christ.

The last stand took place on Mount Andoke [south of Moosh], where some thousand persons had sought refuge. The Kourds were sent in relays to attack them, but for ten or fifteen days were unable to get at them. The soldiers also directed the fire of their mountain guns on them, doing some execution. Finally, after the besieged had been without food for several days, and their ammunition was exhausted, the troops succeeded in reaching the summit without any loss, and let scarcely a man escape.

Now all turned their attention to those who had been driven into the Talvoreeg district. Three or four thousand of the besieged were left in this small plain. When they saw themselves thickly surrounded on all sides by Turks and Kourds, they raised their hands to heaven with an agonizing moan for deliverance. They were thinned out by rifle shots, and the remainder were slaughtered with bayonets and swords, till a veritable river of blood flowed from the heaps of the slain.

And so ended the massacre, for the timely arrival of the Mushire [Commander-in-chief of the Fourth Army Corps at Erzingan] saved a few prisoners alive, and prevented the extermination of four more villages that were on the list to be destroyed, among which was the Protestant village of Havodorick. This was the formidable army the government had massed so many troops and Kourds to vanquish.

So far as is known, not more than ten or fifteen outsiders were among them, and all told it is not likely they had more than one hundred breech-loading rifles.

THE NUMBER OF ARMENIANS SLAIN.

Even if one were able to visit the district, it would be impossible to get more than an approximate estimate of the number of victims, for many were thrown into trenches, which the rain had washed out, and were covered with earth. Where no such trenches existed the bodies were piled up with alternate layers of wood, saturated with kerosene, and set on fire. But it seems certain that the villages of the whole district were wiped out. A Kourdish chief coming late with his men, and finding that there was nothing left for him to do, went off on his own hook and got all the plunder he could from the village of Maineeg, near Havodorick.

A soldier while in quarantine said he had killed five persons, and he had killed less than anybody else. Another confided to one that he had killed a hundred. A soldier got angry while trading with an Armenian the other day in the Bitlis market, and shouted out that they had slain a thousand thousand, and would turn to those in the city next.

It seems safe to say that forty villages were totally destroyed, and it is probable that sixteen thousand at least were killed. *The lowest estimate is ten thousand*, and many put it much higher. This is allowing for more fugitives than it seems possible can have escaped.

To cap the climax, the Governor-General, through imprisonment and intimidation of various kinds, has forced the chief men in all the province (the city of Bitlis alone excepted), to seal an address of gratitude to the Sultan, that the Governor has restored order in the *vilayet* ! !

No. 7.

[The following extract is from a personal letter written by one whose name would be immediately recognized by every reader were we at liberty to make public use of it. The writer is a person of broad influence; but for the present, owing to facts which we are not at liberty to relate, he cannot take a public stand. He will probably be heard from yet.]

F⸺., Nov. 10, 1894.

The massacre which took place a few weeks ago — I do not know the exact date—occurred in the district of Talvoreeg which lies between Moosh and Diabekir. It is an Armenian district, comprising thirty or forty villages, surrounded by Kourds.

Last year some of the Armenians there armed themselves and resisted the Kourds, who are constantly making raids on their villages and carrying off their property. The Governor sent some soldiers, who killed a few Armenians and received a medal from the government for having wiped out a great rebellion. This year there are said to have been ten or fifteen revolutionists among these Armenians. A

Kourdish chief in order to get out of some difficulties that he had gotten into with the government set the ball rolling by carrying off some cattle belonging to certain of the Armenians. The Armenians endeavored to recover the cattle, and a fight followed, in which two Kourds were killed and three were wounded. The Kourds immediately carried their dead to Moosh, laid them down at the government house, reporting that Armenian soldiers were overrunning the land, killing and plundering them.

This furnished the government with the desired excuse for collecting soldiers from far and near. The general is said to have worn on his breast an order from Constantinople, which he read to the soldiers, commanding them to cut down the Armenians root and branch, and adjuring them if they loved their Sultan and their government they would do so. A terrible massacre followed. Between five and ten thousand Christians are said to have been butchered in a most terrible manner. Some soldiers say a hundred fell to each one of them to dispose of; others wept because the Kourds did more execution than they.

No respect was shown to age or sex. Men, women, and infants were treated alike, except that the women were subjected to greater outrage before they were slaughtered. The women were not even granted the privilege of a life of slavery. For example, in one place three or four hundred women, after being forced to serve the vile purposes of a merciless soldiery, were taken to a valley near by and hacked to pieces with sword and bayonet. In another place about two hundred women, weeping and wailing, knelt before the commander and begged for mercy, but the blood-thirsty wretch, after ordering their violation directed the soldiers to dispatch them in a similar manner. In another place a large company, headed by the priest, fell down before the officers saying they had nothing to do with the culprits, and pleading for compassion, but all to no purpose—all were killed. Some sixty young brides and more attractive girls were crowded into a little church in another village, where, after being violated, they were slaughtered, and a stream of human blood flowed from the church door. To some of the more attractive women in one place the proposition was made that they might be spared if they denied their faith. "Why should we deny Christ," they said, and pointing to the dead bodies of their husbands and brothers before them, they nobly answered, "We are no better than they; kill us too,"—and they died.

After the above-mentioned events the Governor attempted to persuade and compel the Armenians to sign a paper thanking the Sultan and himself that justice had been done to the rebels!

No. 8.

[From another city to which soldiers returning brought details of what they had done.]

E . . ., Dec. 6, 1894.

The Armenians, oppressed by Kourds and Turks, said, "We can't pay taxes to both Kourds and the government." Plundered and oppressed by the

Kourds, they resisted them; there were some killed. Then false reports were sent to Constantinople that the Armenians were in arms, in rebellion. Orders were sent to the Mushire [Commander-in-chief] at Erzingan to exterminate them root and branch. The orders read before the army collected in haste from all the chief cities of Eastern Turkey was: "Whoever spares man, woman, or child is disloyal."

The region was surrounded by soldiers of the army and twenty thousand Kourds also are said to have been massed there. Then they advanced upon the centre, driving in the people like a flock of sheep, and continued thus to advance for days. No quarter was given, no mercy shown. Men, women, and children shot down or butchered like sheep. Probably when they were set upon in this way some tried to save their lives and resisted in self-defense. Many who could fled in all directions, but the majority were slain. The most probable estimate is fifteen thousand killed, thirty-five villages plundered, razed, burnt.

Women were outraged and then butchered; a priest taken to the roof of his church and hacked to pieces; young men piled in with wood saturated with kerosene and set on fire; a large number of women and girls collected in church, kept for days, violated by the brutal soldiers, and then murdered. It is said the number was so large that the blood flowed out of the church door. Three soldiers contended over a beautiful girl. They wanted to preserve her, but she too was killed.

Every effort is being made and will be made to falsify (excuse the blots—emblematic of the horrible story) the facts and pull the wool over the eyes of European governments. But the bloody tale will finally be known, the most horrible, it seems to me, that the nineteenth century has known. As a confirmation of the report, the other day several hun-

NAREG: ANCIENT CHURCH AND MODERN HOVELS.

dred soldiers were returning from the seat of war, and at a village near us one was heard to say that he alone with his own hand had killed thirty pregnant women. Some who seem to have some shame for their atrocious deeds say: "What could we do, we were under orders?"

No. 9.

[Later from the same place as the preceding extract. Evidence of a regular soldier who helped dispose of the dead.]

E . . ., Dec. 17, 1894.

The soldiers who went from here talk quite freely about matters at Sassoun. A. heard one talk the other day. He said the work was mostly finished before the E . . . soldiers got there. There was great spoil—flocks, herds, household goods, etc.—but their chief work was to dispose of the heaps and heaps of the dead. The stench was awful. They were gathered into the still standing houses and burned with the houses. They say that the work of destruction was wrought by the *Hamediëh, i. e.*, the newly organized Kourdish regiments. Those regiments are one of the chief elements of danger to the country now.

No. 10.

[From a city some distance from the scene.]

B . . ., Dec. 22, 1894.

You may believe most all that the papers say about the mountains west of Moosh. I wrote you giving you a few more authenticated details. I hope that letter reached you. I give the outline here again. In August the Armenians were declared in rebellion. The regular soldiers and *Hamediëhs* were ordered to the spot. Orders were issued from Constantinople to put down the rebellion. Both regulars and *Hamediёhs* were used. The massacre began after the middle of August—about the 18th—and continued to about the 10th of September. The safe estimates put the number of victims at about four thousand, not less than three thousand five hundred, and, in all probability, more than four thousand.

Men, women, and children were most barbarously slaughtered—unnamable outrages were perpetrated on all. The less horrible outrages were some of the following: bayoneting the men, and in this wounded condition either burying or burning them; outraging women and then dispatching them with bayonets or swords; ripping up pregnant women; impaling infants and children on the bayonet, or dispatching them with the sword; houses fired, and the inmates driven back into the flames.

The unspeakable horror of those three weeks must have sent many a one crazy. The story is told that one soldier found a comely infant and took compassion on it and wished to save it. The mother was found in a crowd of poor, wretched women, but she was raving, calling for her children. She did not recognize the child, and nothing was left to the soldier but to dispatch it.

No. 11.

[Efforts to block the Commission and put the country in shape for inspection by emptying prisons of innocent people.]

B . . ., Dec. 29, 1894.

The Bitlis Governor asks for a cordon on Moosh, as there is cholera reported there. So the Consular Commission is delayed. The Turkish Commission is at Moosh now. Only, the president of it was recalled. In the meantime Sassoun refugees are scattered over the country, begging. Their stories, together with the stories of the soldiers, confirm the most horrible of the reports of cruelty.

In all this, remember that the same thing has been going on on a lesser scale all over the country.

Two weeks ago thirty-six men were dismissed from B . . . prison after three years three months' detention. A little over three years ago three Armenians were most barbarously murdered in the Narman district, north of this city and near the Russian boundary. Some Turks were called up for examination, and all were dismissed. Later, three Turks were murdered and mutilated, apparently in retaliation. The able-bodied men—sixty-two in number—of two villages were thrown into prison. Some of them were condemned to death, some to life imprisonment, and others to various terms of imprisonment. A number of them died—fifteen, I think—in prison. Thirty-six were released the other day, and eleven are still in prison. They have suffered horribly during these three years. In what condition will they find their homes when those who are released return? It is almost certain that none of them knew anything about the murder or had any hand in it. It is said that the murderer is well known, and is in Russia. This case is a Sassoun atrocity on a smaller scale.

For God's sake do not let the public conscience go to sleep again over this reign of terror. The land is almost paralyzed with horror and terror!

No. 12.

[The crisis and the need of keeping the issue clear. The real explanation of the massacre.]

A . ., Jan. 7, 1895.

The importance of the present crisis grows upon me. In the first place Turkey is preparing for a terrible catastrophe by squeezing Armenians, and arming Moslem civilians in Sivas, Aleppo, Castamouni, and other provinces; and in the second place it is putting on the screws tighter everywhere excepting in the three eastern provinces where the Commission is now commencing investigation. In Van and Bitlis the process of arresting and intimidating witnesses went on until the very hour of the departure of the Commission of Investigation. Then the order went out to stop, and those provinces are enjoying the first semblance of quiet that they have known for five years.

This policy of continued massacre and outrage is favored by the profound ignorance which prevails everywhere as to the actual state of things in Turkey. People think that the Sassoun massacre is something exceptional, and that until that is proved there is no evidence of a need of European interference in behalf of Christians in Turkey. What ought to be done is to fix on the mind of the public the fact that Turkey has taken up the policy of crushing the Christians all over the Empire, and has been at it for several years, so that even if the massacre had not taken place, the duty of Europe to prohibit Turkey from acting the part of Anti-Christ was still self-evident.

No. 13.

[Turks getting nervous, but not enough to forget taxes.]

B . . ., Jan. 5, 1895.

The horrible stories are only being confirmed. It is said that unborn babes were cut from their quivering mothers and carried about on spear tops. The Turks themselves now see that they went a step too far, and they are feeling the awful tension of suspense as much as the Christians. However, the pitiless collection of taxes is causing fearful suffering.

No. 14.

[Prospects of the Commission of Inquiry, and its inadequacy in any case to do justice to the chronic state of the country.]

B . . ., Jan. 12, 1895.

The people are in a state of horror because of the massacre. The Commission has been expected for some time, and without doubt the local authorities have used every means to cover up their tracks and terrorize still further those who may be probable witnesses. Those who are encouraged to testify will be again at the mercy of the Turks after the Commission rises. I have not the slightest doubt that some will be courageous enough to testify, but it will be at great odds. Almost everything is against the perfect success of the Commission's work, or rather the favorable outcome of the work of the European delegates. It will not be right to stake the fate of Armenia on the outcome of the work of this Commission.

Rather it should be remembered that Sassoun is the outcome of a governmental system. There have been hundreds of Sassouns all over the country all through the last ten years, as you know. The laxity of Europe has afforded opportunity for the merciless working of this system in all its vigor. It is born of religious and race hatred, and has in mind the crushing of Christianity and Christians.

It is not the Kourdish robbers, or famine, or cholera that have to answer for the present state of the country. It is rather the robbery, and famine, and worse than cholera entailed on the country by the workings of this system. It is not alone the blood of five thousand men, women, children, and babies, that rises in a fearful wail to heaven, calling for just vengeance, but also the fearful suffering, the desolate homes, the wanton cruelty of tax collectors and petty officials, and the violated honor of scores and scores.

The Turk is on trial. Let not Sassoun alone go in evidence, but remember that the same wail rises from all over the country.

[Evidence of an eye-witness, whose occupation saved him. Very few succeeded in escaping to tell the tale.]

I saw an eye-witness to some of the Sassoun destruction. He passed through three villages. They were all in ruins, and mutilated bodies told the horrible tale. For four or five days he was in one village. During the day parties of the scattered inhabitants would come in and throw themselves upon the mercy of the officer in command. About two hours after sundown each evening these prisoners of that day were marched out of camp to a neighboring valley, and the air was rent with their pitiful cries. He saw nothing more of them. He estimates that five hundred men disappeared in that way while he was there.

Between two hundred and three hundred women and children were brought into camp. They also disappeared, how he did not know. He was an Armenian muleteer pressed for the transport of the military. He was sent out of the district to Moosh. He and his companion are the only eye-witnesses we have seen.

Another refugee from a village on the border tells the story of how his mother, after terrible hardships, escaped to a monastery where this young man was a servant. She told of the merciless slaughter of all the rest of the household, and destruction of the village. She with her young child succeeded in reaching the monastery, where after a few days she died of her wounds.

A Chapter of Horrors.

The country waits breathlessly the result of the investigation. May the Lord of nations stretch forth His almighty arm to save!

No. 15.

B   ., Jan. 25, 1895.

Eight to ten thousand breaths gone out is about enough, but the form beggars description. Some impaled, some buried alive, some burned in houses with the help of kerosene, pregnant women ripped up, children seized by the hair to have the head lopped off as if it were a worthless bud, hundreds of women turned over to the vile soldiery with sequence of terrible slaughter.

No. 16.

[The last letter was written in this country by one who has spent years in the very heart of the afflicted region.]

NEW YORK, Jan. 25, 1895.

Up to May, 1894, when I left Van, the whole Christian population of that region was simply paralyzed by fear, and there was no manifestation of any revolutionary thought or intention by the Armenians. Certainly, if such a revolution were contemplated, you would expect to find it in the Van and Bitlis *vilayets* [provinces], where the provocation is the greatest.

[Many other letters have been received which contain no new evidence, but which in every particular confirm what is here reported. It would add nothing to the evidence to give further extracts here.

Many who have given no reports, but knowing that some others have done so, say: "You can safely believe all, and more, for the sickening details that come in are becoming worse and worse." "No report can be exaggerated as to the horrible event," etc., etc.

All the sixteen preceding extracts, and the original letters from which they are taken, are endorsed by the twenty names which are reproduced in facsimile on pages 2 and 4. The following additional letters, which have arrived too late to be submitted with the above, have come through the same channels and are of equal weight.]

No. 17.

[This is an extract from a letter written from a town in the province of Erzroom, and has no connection with the Sassoun affair. It is the written testimony of a pure, sensitive Christian woman, who is only one of hundreds that have been and are being trodden in the mire of Moslem lust. It was intended for the eye of a beloved teacher of the poor victim who wrote it. If it is wrong for me to publish it to the world, let God and the reader judge. Remember that the silence of death reigns in Sassoun, and that

A Chapter of Horrors.

throughout other regions terror paralyzes the tongue. It bears date, November 4, 1894, Old Style (*i. e.*, November 16th). It is eloquent in its agonizing pathos, and shows the condition of the country in which such events are common occurrences, and against which there is no redress.]

ARMENIAN GIRLS OF VAN.

[Translated.]

G——., Nov. 4, 1894.

"*I implore and earnestly entreat that you will remember one of your former pupils, and hear my cry for sympathy and protection. I have been outraged. Oh, woe is me, eternal pain and sorrow to my young heart! Evil disposed and lawless men have robbed me of the bloom and beauty of my wifely purity. It was H—— Bey, the son of the Kaimakam (the local*

Turkish Governor residing in the village). It was in the evening between six and seven o'clock. I was engaged in my household work. I stepped outside the door, when I suddenly found myself in the grasp of four men. They smothered my cries and threatened my life, and by force carried me off to a strange house. Oh, what black hours were those till the sweet light of the sun once more arose! Though this is written with ink, believe me, it is written in blood and tears."

No. 18.

[The following letter was written from an entirely different part of Turkey from the preceding letters. It is a region far remote from the massacres, and yet indicates a state of affairs that is deplorable. The writer is not an American nor is he a native of Turkey; he has spent several years in that country and is a man in whom all would have the highest confidence were we at liberty to give the name.]

H . ., Jan. 11, 1895.

Those cordons and quarantine, together with the extraordinary precautions, taken by the hitherto immovable Turk, with regard to cholera that was still far away and in an entirely different direction, were a mystery to all, although every person knew that the ostensible purpose was not the real one. Now that the tidings from Moosh have come in, the mystery of the series of cordons between here and Harpoot is explained. There is very strong evidence that a general massacre or a series of massacres of Christians has been understood by the local governments to be the order of the day. It is not likely that a definite order to that effect has been given out from the Capitol, but multitudes of recent events go to show that the everlasting persecutions and annoyances, and the methods used in past times to grind down the Christians, have come to be regarded as insufficient. Everywhere there is an activity, a watchfulness, and an energy displayed by the government in the recent efforts to encompass the Christians and to cut off their name and existence, that point to a newly formed plan to be put into execution with as little waste of time as possible. Woe to the poor remnant in this land if the European and American governments disregard recent events in Turkey! Christian nations in that case, even if they do not directly participate in what will certainly follow sooner or later, cannot be held guiltless of the blood of their fellow-men. . . .

Another case in which I was concerned has gone the same way. Last spring a Protestant woman in Y. was assaulted and violated by three Turks. They were tried in F. and found guilty; but that infamous court in S., under the influence of the still more infamous *Mutesarif* (Governor), having recently reviewed the case, reversed the original judgment and released the guilty. There is no remedy. No appeal can be made. The only thing that can be done is to prosecute the court in S., but that, in the present state of things, would be utterly useless. The result will be that such crimes will become more frequent than ever—the perpetrators feeling confident that there is very little likelihood of punishment being meted out to them.

The government pretends to look with special suspicion on H. just now. The *Vali* (Governor-General) claims there are secret societies here. I told him there is nothing of the kind in H. now. The poor people are afraid to open their mouths or to go out of their houses. You can scarcely conceive the change that has come over the people within the past few months. Terror and amazement have taken hold of them to such an extent as to become manifest in their countenances even. All arms and weapons are being taken from the people here these days.

The *Kaimakam* (local Governor) and other officers walk the streets and the K. road every night. Attempts have been made by officers and soldiers to draw Christians into a quarrel, but they have hitherto failed. One night this week, the *Commissaire* (Chief of Police) without any provocation fired three times at a Christian, but the other offered no resistance. Moslem officers are taking possession of the property of Christians and doing just as they please without regard to law or justice. . . .

The church and school in O. have been closed and for two months now the people have not been allowed to come together for worship. They are forbidden even to have prayers offered in their houses.

CHAPTER II.

GENERAL INFORMATION ABOUT EASTERN TURKEY.

IN order that the ordinary reader may grasp the situation in Armenia, information is given at this point in regard to the country itself, its administration, the elements that compose the population, and their relations to one another.

The massacre took place in the mountainous Sassoun district just south of Moosh, two days' ride west of Bitlis, a large city where the Provincial-Governor and a permanent military force reside. It is near the western end of Lake Van, about eight hundred miles east of Constantinople, two hundred and fifty miles south of Trebizond on the Black Sea, and only one hundred and fifty miles from the Russian and Persian frontiers of Asiatic Turkey. These distances do not seem great until the difficulties of travel are considered. The roads are, in most cases, bridle paths, impassable for vehicles, without bridges, infested with highwaymen, and unprovided with lodging-places. It is, therefore, necessary to go to the expense of hiring government guards, and to burden oneself with all articles likely to be needed on the way—tents, food supplies, cooking utensils, beds, etc., which also imply cooks, baggage horses, and grooms. Thus equipped, it is possible, after obtaining the necessary government permits, often a matter of vexatious delay, to move about the country. The ordinary rate is from twenty to thirty miles a day. With a good horse and no baggage I have gone three hundred and fifty miles, from Harpoot to Van, in eight days, but that was quite exceptional. In spring, swollen streams and mud; in summer, oppressive heat; and in winter, storms, are serious impediments. In the neighborhood of Bitlis the telegraph poles are sometimes buried, and horses cannot be taken out of the stables on account of the snow. The mails are often weeks behind, both in arriving and departing, and even Turkish lightning seems to be *yavash*, and crawl sluggishly along the wires.

Turkish Armenia—by the way, "Armenia" is a name prohibited in Turkey—is a large plateau quadrangular in shape, and sixty thousand square miles in area, about the size of Iowa. It is bounded on the north by the Russian frontier, a line from the Black Sea to Mount Ararat, by Persia on the east, the Mesopotamian plain on the south, and Asia Minor on the west. It contains about six hundred thousand Armenians, which is only one fourth the number found in all Turkey. The surface is rough, consisting of valleys and plains from four to six thousand feet above sea-level, broken and shut in by bristling peaks and mountain ranges, from ten to seventeen thousand feet high, as in the case of Ararat. Ancient Armenia greatly varied in extent at different epochs, reaching to the Caspian at one time, and even bordering on the Mediterranean Sea during the Crusades. It included the Southern Caucasus, which now contains a large, growing, prosperous, and happy Armenian population under the Czar, whose government allows them the free exercise of their ancestral religion, and admits them to many high civil and military positions. The Armenians now number about four million, of whom two million five hundred thousand are in Turkey, one million two hundred and fifty thousand in Russia, one hundred and fifty thousand in Persia and other parts of Asia, one hundred thousand scattered through Europe, and five thousand in the United States.

The scenery, while harsh, owing to the lack of verdure, is on a grand scale. Around the shores of the great Van Lake are many views of entrancing beauty. The climate is temperate and the atmosphere brilliant and stimulating. It is a dry, treeless region, but fertile under irrigation, and abounding in mineral wealth, including coal. Owing to primitive methods of agriculture, and to danger while reaping and even planting crops, only a small part is under cultivation, and frequent famines are the result. The mineral resources are entirely untouched, because the Turks lack both capital and brains to develop them, and prevent foreigners from doing it lest this might open the door for further European inspection and interference with their methods of administering the country.

All local authority is practically in the hands of the *Valis*, provincial governors, who are sent from

Constantinople to represent the sovereign, and are accountable to him alone. The blind policy which was inaugurated by the present Sultan of dismissing non-Moslems from every branch of public service— post, telegraph, custom-house, internal revenue, engineering, and the like—has already been carried out to a large extent all over the empire, and especially in Armenia. The frequent changes in Turkish officials keeps their business in a state of "confusion worse confounded," and incites them to improve their chance to plunder while it lasts. Traces of the relatively large revenue, wrung from the people, and spent in improvements of service to them, are very hard to find.

THE INHABITANTS.

Probably about one half of the population of Turkish Armenia is Mohammedan, composed of Turks and Kurds. The former are mostly found in and near the large cities, such as Erzingan, Baibourt, Erzerum, and Van, and the plains along the northern part. The Kurds live in their mountain villages over the whole region. The term Kurdistan, which in this region the Turkish Government is trying to substitute for the historical one Armenia, has no political or geographical propriety except as indicating the much larger area over which the Kurds are scattered. In this vague sense it applies to a stretch of mountainous country about fifteen hundred miles in length, starting between Erzingan and Malatiah, and sweeping east and south over into Persia as far as Kermanshah.

A KURD OF THE OLD TYPE.

The number of the Kurds is very uncertain. Neither Sultan nor Shah has ever attempted a census of them; and as they are very indifferent taxpayers, the revenue tables—wilfully distorted for political purposes—are quite unreliable. From the estimates of British consular officers there appear to be about one and a half million Turkish Kurds, of whom about 600,000 are in the *vilayets* of Erzroom, Van, and Bitlis, and the rest in the *vilayets* of Harpoot, Diarbekir, Mosul, and Bagdad. This is a very liberal estimate. There are also supposed to be about 750,000 in Persia.[1]

The Kurds, whose natural instincts lead them to a pastoral and predatory life, are sedentary or nomad according to local and climatic circumstances. Where exposed to a severe mountain winter they live exclusively in villages, and in the case of Bitlis have even formed a large part of the city population. But the tribes in the south, who have access to the Mesopotamian plains, prefer a migratory life, oscillating with the season between the lowlands and the mountains. The sedentary greatly outnumber the nomad Kurds, but the latter are more wealthy, independent, and highly esteemed. There is, probably, little ethnic distinction between the two classes.

A fourteenth-century list of Kurdish tribes contains many names identical with those of powerful families who claim a remote ancestry. " There was, up to a recent period, no more picturesque or interesting scene to be witnessed in the East than the court of one of these great Kurdish chiefs, where, like another Saladin, [who was a Kurd himself,] the bey ruled in

[1] *Encyc. Britannica,* " Kurdistan."

patriarchal state, surrounded by hereditary nobility, regarded by his clansmen with reverence and affection, and attended by a body-guard of young Kurdish warriors, clad in chain armor, with flaunting silken scarfs, and bearing javelin, lance, and sword as in the time of the crusaders."[1] Within two days' ride southeast of Van, I found the ruins of four massive Kurdish castles at Shaddakh, Norduz, Bashkallah, and Khoshab, which must have rivalled those of the feudal barons on the Rhine. The Armenian and Nestorian villagers were much better off as serfs of the powerful masters of these strongholds than as the victims of Kurdish plunder and of Ottoman taxation and oppression which they now are.

The Kurds are naturally brave and hospitable, and, in common with many other Asiatic races, possess certain rude but strict feelings of honor. But since their power has been broken by the Turks, their castles ruined, and their chiefs exiled, these finer qualities and more chivalrous sentiments have also largely disappeared under the principle of *noblesse oblige* reversed. In most regions they have degenerated into a wild, lawless set of brigands, proud, treacherous, and cruel. The traditions of their former position and power serve only to feed their hatred of the Turks who caused their fall, and their jealousy and contempt of the Christians who have been for generations their serfs, whose progress and increase they cannot tolerate.

One who has a taste for adventure and is willing to take his life in his hands, can find among them as

[1] *Encyc. Britannica*, "Kurdistan."

fine specimens of the human animal as are to be found anywhere—sinewy, agile, and alert, with a steady penetrating eye as cool, cold, and cruel as that

RUINS OF A KURDISH CASTLE AT KHOSHAB.

of a tiger. I vividly recollect having just this impression under circumstances analogous to that of a hunter who suddenly finds himself face to face with a lord of the jungle. There was no sense of fear, at the time, but rather a keen delight and fascination in watching the magnificent creature before me. His thin aquiline face, his neck and hands were stained by the weather to a brown as delicate as that of a meerschaum pipe, and on his broad exposed breast the thick growth of hair obliterated any impression of nudeness. For a few moments he seemed engaged in some sinister calculation, but at last quietly moved away. Perhaps he wanted only a cigarette. Perhaps he wondered if I, too, had claws. The Winchester rifle behind his back did not escape my notice, nor did the gun across my saddle escape his. It is hardly necessary to remind those who may desire such experiences as the above, that the usual retinue of cooks, servants, and *zabtiéhs* should be dispensed with in order to secure the best opportunities for observation.

The Kurdish costumes, always picturesque, show much local variation in cut and color. The beys and khans of the colder north almost invariably prefer broadcloth, and find the finest fabrics and richest shades—specially imported for them—none too good. But the loose flowing garments of the Sheikhs and wealthy Kocher nomads of the south are often very inexpensive, and suggest Arab simplicity and dignity. There is, no doubt, considerable Arab blood in some of these families, who refer to the fact with pride.

The women of the Kurds, contrary to usual Mohammedan custom, go unveiled and have large liberty, but there is no reason to suspect their virtue. Their prowess, also, is above reproach, and rash would be the man, Turk or Christian, who would venture to invade the mountain home when left in charge of its female defenders. On the whole, the Kurds are a race of fine possibilities, far superior to the North American Indian, to whom they are often ignorantly compared. Under a just, intelligent, and firm government much might be expected of them in time.

They keep up a strict tribal relation, owing allegiance to their Sheikhs, some of whom are still strong and rich, and engage in bitter feuds with one another. They could not stand a moment against the Ottoman power if determined to crush and disarm them. But three years ago His Majesty summoned the chiefs to the capital, presented them with decorations, banners, uniforms, and military titles, and sent them back to organize their tribes into cavalry regiments, on whom he was pleased to bestow the name *Hamedieh*, after his own. Thus, shrewdly appealing to their pride of race, and winking at their subsequent acts, the Sultan obtained a power eager in time of peace to crush Armenian growth and spirit, and a bulwark that might check, in his opinion, the first waves of the next dreaded Russian invasion. In the last war the Kurdish contingent was worse than useless as was shown by Mr. Norman,[1] of the *London Times*.

The Armenians, a very important element of the population, are generally known as being bright, practical, industrious, and moral. They are of a very peaceable disposition, and entirely unskilled in the use of arms, the mere possession of which

[1] *Armenia and the Campaign of 1877.*

is a serious crime in the case of Christians, although the Kurds are well equipped with modern rifles and revolvers, and always carry them. Their great and fundamental weakness, seen through all their history, is a lack of coherence, arising from their exaggerated individualism. They have the distinction of being the first race who accepted Christianity, King Dertad receiving baptism in 276 A. D., thirty-seven years before Constantine ventured to issue even the Edict of Toleration. Their martyr roll has grown with every century. The fact that the Armenian stock exists at all to-day, is proof of its wonderful vitality and excellent quality. For three thousand years Armenia, on account of her location, has been trampled into dust both by devastating armies and by migrating hordes. She has been the prey of Nebuchadnezzar, Xerxes, and Alexander; of the Romans, the Parthians, and Persians; of Byzantine, Saracen, and Crusader; of Seljuk and Ottoman, and Russian and Kurd. Through this awful record, the Christian church founded by Gregory, "The Illuminator," has been the one rallying point and source of strength, and this explains the tremendous power of the Cross on the hearts of all, even of the most ignorant peasant.

CHAPTER III.

THE CHRONIC CONDITION OF ARMENIA AND KURDISTAN.

MANY statements in regard to the state of affairs in Eastern Turkey are criticised as being too sweeping and general, and the inference is drawn that they are exaggerations, not based on exact knowledge of the facts. This chapter will, therefore, contain nothing but definite incidents and figures, names and places also being added regardless of consequences. This information is furnished by a trustworthy authority on the ground, and has already been published in *The Independent*, of New York, January 17, 1895, from which I quote verbatim. It shows the usual course of things in times of so-called peace between Kurds and their Christian slaves, and indicates to what sort of a life these Armenian, Jacobite, and Nestorian Christians are condemned when no massacre is in hand. From my own residence and travels in Armenia, I know that the incidents related would apply to hundreds of villages with simply a change of name.

"*A Partial List of Exactions made upon the Village of Mansurich of Bohtan* (Kaimakamlik of Jezireh) by the government, and by Mustapha Pasha, a Kurdish Kocher, or nomad chief, in 1893:

SUMMARY.

1. Government Exaction	Excess of official demand	3,000 ps.[1]	
	Amount of double tax	4,000	
	Produce taken by gendarmes	2,000	9,000 ps.
2. Exaction by M. Pasha.	Excess of tithe revenue	1,500	
	Damage to crops	2,000	3,500

Total excess taken from village for 1893......... 12,500
Total of legitimate taxes on village for the year... 14,000

The village complained to the government of Mustapha Pasha's exactions, but no redress was given by the government, nor anything done to Mustapha Pasha, who, when he learned of their having made complaint, sent droves of sheep to devour the crops that remained, viz., five pieces of ground sown and bearing cotton, millet, flaxseed, etc., valued at 2000 piasters."

"*Partial List of Exaction by Aghas of Shernakh* (one day north of Jezireh), from Hassana of Bohtan, during years 1891–'93. Hassana has sixty houses:

```
1893.
Use of 30 men to carry flour for Mohammed
    Agha, 2 days.............................. 150 ps.
For Mohammed Agha, cash 10 liras............. 1,000
    "          "        "  15 pieces of cloth........ 150
"   Taher Agha, cash 14 liras................. 1,400
    "   "    "   taken from village priest, cash
                 75 ps., saddle 75 ps., watch
                 200 ps..................... 350
"   Sahdoon Agha, cash 2 liras................ 200
"   Mohammed............................... 120
                                              ─────
         Carried forward.................... 3,370 ps.
```

[1] A piastre is a Turkish coin of about five cents, or two pence-half penny. In this region the pay of a day laborer is from two to five piastres.

			Brought forward	3,370 ps.
	For Khorsheed			57
"	Mohammed Agha,		harvest, 500 men at 3 ps..	1,500
"	"	"	repair of his roads, 65 men, 3 days	487
"	"	"	repair of his roads, 50 men, 3 days	375
"	"	"	preparation of boiled wheat for winter, 450 men and 14 animals	1,160
"	"	"	building house in Dader, 150 men	375
"	"	"	2000 ceiling sticks, 10 posts	554
"	"	"	4 large trees for rafters, at 50 ps	200
	Total for 1893			8,078 ps.

The above were noted in a book at the time of the occurrence by a village priest, as being seen by him personally, and do not give the great part of the exactions of the Shernakh Kurds, which he did not see.

One item additional to above: all the cotton of Mohammed Agha of Shernakh is, by the villagers, beaten, spun, twisted, woven, and returned as cloth (involving many days' labor and two days' journey), and any weight lost in the making up the amount must be made good.

This oppression is increasing from year to year. The above priest noted for years 1880-'82, taken by Aghas—cash, 4141 ps.; 90 animals used, 450 ps.; 314 men used, 785 ps. Total for three years, 5376, as over against 10,973 ps. for three years, 1891-'93."

"Testimony given in writing, by a Christian of the District of Berwer, in reference to the oppression of Christians in that district by the Kurds, of which he himself was an eye-witness, the examples given being confined to three small villages and of recent occurrence. He gives the names of places and of the parties concerned, both Kurds and Christians. We summarize them.

Murders.—Eight men mentioned by name, others generalized.

Robbery.—Cash, 9 liras; again 10 liras; again 15 liras; smaller sums being taken continually.

Mohammed Beg, of Berwer, and his relatives responsible in greater part for the above; also for robbing of two houses in Ina D'Noony.

For generations these Christians have sown the fields of these Kurds, harvested them, done their threshing, irrigated their fields, cut and brought in the grass as fodder for the sheep for use during the winter, together with much other labor, and all without recompense, they finding themselves.

(These things are accompanied, of course, with cursings and beatings.)"

"A number of Christian villages lying farther back in the mountains are even more severely oppressed. The people are literally bought and sold as slaves. In other districts the buying and selling of Christians by Kurds is common."

"Village of Shakh (five hours from Jezireh); like Mansurieh deserted for months by reason of extortion by tax collectors. Many of the people lived during the winter in caves in the mountains."

"The writer was in Nahrwan when the Kaimakam of Jezireh came, several weeks after a murder, to examine into it. The examination was rendered so oppressive to the Christians that the people were glad to declare that nothing had happened, in order to escape any further inquisition. Even the old mother of the murdered man was frightened until she declared that she did not know of any such occurrence, and had no complaints to make against anybody."

"Kannybalaver—Kaimakamlik of Amadia. During the years 1893–'94 this village was raided several times by the Gugier and Sendier Kurds of the Kaimakamlik of Jezireh. They took one hundred head of animals, field tools, household utensils, beds, wool and yarn, gall-nuts—all of their fall gathering,—and dry goods which had been brought in to sell. At their last visit everything movable was carried off, and the people deserted the village. A leading man of the village, Gegoo by name, was seized by the Kurds, carried for several miles, and was then murdered in cold blood. There were about one hundred Kurds in the band led by Ahrno, brother of Hassu of Ukrul and Kerruvanu. The chief men of their village are Sherriffu and Hassu, who would be responsible for such a raid."

"In the city of Mosul, where there is a Vali, Christians are robbed and killed openly. Three cases are given. Last year a young man, of the Protestant community, of high standing in the city as a merchant, was standing before his door when two young Kurds of notorious character came along, and one of them, without the slightest provocation, at the time or previously, from mere wantonness, stabbed him, and would have killed him had he not been restrained. The family of the man, though one of the most influential families among the Christians of the city, did not dare to make accusation against him, knowing that the only result would be more bloodshed."

"An old missionary who has been familiar with the region from Bohtan to Amadia for years, says these oppressions are increasing, and unless something is done speedily, all the Christian villages of these various districts will soon fall into the hands of the Kurds just as they have in Zabur."

"These instances of oppression given are but a few of the many which might be given. Indeed it is not these greater occurrences, as the big raids and murders, which are the most serious to the Christian. It is the daily constant exactions and oppressions which are crushing the life out of them."

A whole chapter might well be devoted to the oppression by government officials in assessing and collecting taxes. This evil is general, affecting all Turkey. A brief summary of these abuses as generally practised will be given. In view of the poverty-stricken condition of the land, even the legitimate taxes are an exceedingly heavy burden on Moslem and Christian alike, but the burden is greatly increased by the methods here classified:

SUMMARY OF ABUSES.

"I. *Unjust and corrupt assessments.*

1. Villagers are compelled to give assessors presents of money to prevent them from over estimating the taxable persons and property.

2. Assessors, to secure additional bribes, signify their willingness to make an underestimate. This, in turn, affords opportunity for blackmail, which is used by succeeding officials."

"II. *Injustice and severity in collecting.*

1. The collectors, like the assessors, have ways of extorting presents and bribes from the people.

2. The collectors, as a rule, go to the villages on Sunday, as on that day they find the people in the village. They frequently interrupt the Christian services, and show disrespect to their churches or places of prayer.

3. The collection of the taxes is accompanied with unnecessary abuse and reviling, sometimes even with wanton destruction of property.

4. Disregard of impoverished condition of people. Even after several failures of crops in succession, when famine was so severe that the people were many of them being fed by foreign charity, the taxes were collected in full and with severity.

Their food supply, beds, household utensils, and farming implements were seized by the collectors in lieu of taxes. Many were compelled to borrow money at enormous rates of interest, mortgaging their fields and future crops. Unscrupulous officials and other Kurds, in whose interests such opportunities are created, thus became possessed of Christian villages, the people of which henceforth becoming practically slaves to them.

5. These collectors make false returns of taxes received. The official in the city is secured by a bribe, and the matter is kept quiet until a succeeding set of officials come into office. They send their officers to the villages to present claims for back taxes. The villagers in vain contend that they have paid them. They have no receipts. They do not

dare to ask for them. Or the head man of the village who keeps the account has been bribed to falsify his accounts. These taxes are collected again, entailing much suffering upon the people.

6. The books in the government offices at the Kaimakamlik are often incorrect through mistakes or dishonesty, and in consequence taxes are paid on fictitious names or on persons who have been dead for years."

"III. *Farming of taxes.*

Taxes are often farmed out to the highest bidder, who usually is some powerful Kurdish chief. Either in consequence of his power, or by means of bribes, he is secure from interference on the part of the government. He collects the amount due the government and then takes for himself as much as he chooses, his own will or an exhausted threshing-floor being the only limit to his rapacity.

While he is collector for these villages they are considered as belonging to him. During the year his followers pay frequent visits to the villages. They are ignorant and brutal, and on such visits, as also when collecting taxes, they treat the villagers with the utmost severity."

"IV. All the above assessors and collectors—and they are many, a different one for each kind of tax, personal, house and land, sheep, tobacco, etc.—on their visits to the villages, take with them *a retinue of servants and soldiers, who, with their horses, must be kept at the expense of the village, thus entailing a very heavy additional burden upon them.* Soldiers and servants sent to the villagers to make collections, very naturally take something for themselves."

All the preceding testimony refers to regions where Jacobite and Nestorian Christians predominate and thus prove that Armenians are by no means the only sufferers.

The same state of affairs was found by Mrs. Bishop, who made investigations on the ground five years ago.

"On the whole, the same condition of alarm prevails among the Armenians as I witnessed previously among the Syrian[1] *rayahs*. It is more than alarm, it is *abject terror*, and not without good reason. In plain English, general lawlessness prevails over much of this region. Caravans are stopped and robbed, travelling is, for Armenians, absolutely unsafe, sheep and cattle are being driven off, and outrages, which it would be inexpedient to narrate, are being perpetrated. Nearly all the villages have been reduced to extreme poverty, while at the same time they are squeezed for the taxes which the Kurds have left them without the means of paying.

The repressive measures which have everywhere followed 'the Erzerum troubles' of last June [1890] —the seizure of arms, the unchecked ravages of the Kurds, the threats of the Kurdish Beys, who are boldly claiming the sanction of the government for their outrages, the insecurity of the women, and a dread of yet worse to come — have reduced these peasants to a pitiable state."[2]

---

[1] Often called Nestorian.

[2] Mrs. Isabella Bird Bishop, *Journeys in Persia and Kurdistan*, vol. ii., p. 374, 375.

Through the influence of the British Ambassador at Constantinople Mrs. Bishop was allowed to state the situation to the Grand Vizier in person, and on arriving in England she presented a detailed statement of facts to the Foreign Office and also to a Parliamentary Committee.

That the recent outrages in Sassoun are conspicuous by their extent rather than character, the following incident, which came within the author's own knowledge, on the ground at the time, will show. In June, 1893, four young Armenians and their wives, living only two miles from the city of Van, where the Governor and a large military force reside, were picking herbs on the hillside. They carefully kept together and intended to return before night. They were observed by a band of passing Kurds, who, in broad daylight, fell upon the defenceless party, butchered the young men, and, as to the brides, it is needless to relate further. The villagers going out the next day found the four bodies, not simply dead, but slashed and disfigured almost beyond recognition. They resolved to make a desperate effort to let their wrongs at least be known.

Hastily yoking up four rude ox carts, they placed on each the naked remains of one of the victims, with his distracted widow sitting by the side, shorn of her hair in token of dishonor. This gruesome procession soon reached the outskirts of the city, where it was met by soldiers sent to turn it back. The unarmed villagers offer no resistance, but declare their readiness to perish if not heard. The soldiers shrink from extreme measures that might cause trouble among the thirty thousand Armenians of Van, who are now rapidly gathering about the scene. The Turkish bayonets retreat before the bared breasts of the villagers. With ever increasing numbers, but without tumult, the procession passed before the doors of the British and Russian Vice-Consulates, of the Persian Consul-General, the Chief of Police and other high officials, till it paused before the great palace of the Governor.

At this point Bahri Pasha, who is still Governor, stuck his head out of the second-story window and said: "I see it. Too bad! Take them away and bury them. I will do what is necessary." Within two days some Kurds were brought in, among whom were several who were positively identified by the women; but, upon their denying the crime, they were immediately released and escaped. The utter hopelessness of securing any justice was so apparent, and experience had so often demonstrated the danger of arousing the Kurds to greater atrocity by further efforts to punish them, that the case was dropped and soon forgotten in the callousness produced by other cases of frequent occurrence. The system of mail inspection is so effective (all letters of subjects must be handed in open at the post-office) and the danger of reporting is so great that I doubt that any account of this incident has ever been given to the civilized world. This case was doubtless reported by the former British Vice-Consul, unless he was busy hunting, and, as usual, was buried in the archives of the Foreign Office for "state reasons."

A foreign physician, never a missionary, and now

out of the country, told me that during a large practice of a year and a half in Armenia, while using every effort to save life, only one case was remembered of regret by the doctor for a fatal ending,—so sad is the lot of those who survive. This instance will explain the strange statement. A call came to see a young man sent home from prison in a dying condition. He could not speak, and had to be nourished for days by artificial feeding, because his stomach could not retain food. Constant and skilful care for a month brought him back to life, from the condition to which his vile, dark, unventilated cell and scanty food had brought him. As soon as the police learned of his unexpected recovery, he was seized and re-imprisoned, though an only son, with a widowed mother and sister dependent upon him. When last heard of, he was still "awaiting trial." Such confinement is a favorite method of intimidation and blackmail in the case of the innocent, and, in the case of the guilty, amounts to punishment without the cost and labor involved in proving the guilt and securing sentence by legal process.

From my own house in Van goods of considerable value were stolen in November, 1893. Though I had good clews to the guilty parties and would have been glad to recover my property, I felt constrained to use every precaution *not* to let the affair come to the ears of the police, lest they should use it as a pretext for searching the houses of many innocent Armenians, in the hope of finding a letter, book, or weapon of some kind, which might serve as an excuse for imprisonment. This course exposed me to further attacks of thieves and necessitated a night watchman.

WHY ARE THESE FACTS NOT KNOWN?

The ignorance and incredulity of the public is a most significant commentary on the situation. But the explanation is simple. In the nature of the case, in reports of outrages where the victims or their friends are still within the clutches of the Turks, all names of individuals and often the exact locality must be concealed. Such anonymous accounts naturally arouse little interest, and, of course, cannot be verified. The former British Consul-General at Erzerum, Mr. Clifford Lloyd, showed me at that place many such reports sent to him by members of Parliament for verification. He was unable to verify them, but said that the reports gave a correct impression of the condition of the country. At that very time, October, 1890, Mr. Lloyd called attention, in an official dispatch, published in the "*Blue Books*," to:

"1. The insecurity of the lives and properties of the Armenians. 2. The insecurity of their persons, and the absence of all liberty of thought and action. 3. The unequal status held by the Christian as compared with the Mussulman in the eyes of the government."

On this subject there are five channels of varying market value. First. Consular reports, meagre and often inaccessible. The United States has no consuls in Armenia, and consequently no "official" knowledge of its condition. European consuls are expected to report nothing that they are not absolutely sure of, and are given to understand, both by their own governments and by that of Turkey, that they must not make themselves obnoxious in seeking information. They are, at best, passive until their aid is sought, and then alarm the suppliants by refusing to touch the case unless allowed to use names. Second. Missionaries, whose mouths are sealed. They would be the best informed and most trustworthy witnesses. But they feel it their first duty to safeguard the great benevolent and educational interests committed to them by not exciting the suspicion and hostility of the government. Their position is a delicate one, conditional on their neutrality, like that of officers of the Red Cross Society in war. Third. Occasional travellers, whose first impressions are also often their last and whose hasty jottings are likely to be very interesting and may be very misleading. Not so in the case of Mrs. Isabella Bird Bishop, whom I had the pleasure of meeting there, and who embodied the result of her careful investigations in an article entitled, "The Shadow of the Kurd" in *The Contemporary Review*.[1] Fourth. Much evidence from Armenian sources, which is often unjustly discredited as being the exaggeration, if not fabrication, of "revolutionists who seek a political end." Fifth. Turkish official reports, often obtained by corrupt or violent means, or invented to suit the circumstances. Though the financial credit of the Ottoman Government was long ago exhausted, there are some well meaning people who still place confidence in Turkish explanations and promises.

[1] *The Contemporary Review*, May and June, 1891.

WHAT CAN BE DONE?

The scope of this book does not permit a discussion of even the Armenian phase of the Eastern question, beyond a bare reference to its possible three-fold solution. There is, first, Russian annexation, a step for which the sufferers themselves are praying, and which Russia is prepared to execute at a moment's notice. If this were the only alternative from present conditions, it should be universally welcomed. Russia is crude, stupid, and, in certain aspects, brutal, but she is not decrepit, debauched, and doting like official Turkey. The diseases of the "Sick Man" are incurable and increasing, while the bully of the North is young, of good blood, and with an energy suggestive of a force of nature. Russia shaves half the head of seceders from the Orthodox Church and transports them. Turkey, with more tact, quietly "disposes" of converts from Islam, many of whom would step forth if the prospect were less than death. The Jewish question, from the Russian standpoint, is largely a social and industrial one, like the Chinese question in the United States. When the writer passed from Turkish Armenia into the Caucasus, it was from a desert to a garden; from danger to perfect security; from want and sorrow to plenty and cheer.

Until lately, thousands of Turkish Armenians have been in the habit of crossing the Russian border in spring, earning good wages during the summer, and returning to spend the winter with their families. This has opened their eyes to the contrast between the two lands and turned their hearts to Russia.

The second solution is Armenian autonomy, like that of Bulgaria, the fond dream of those who ignore the geographical difficulties, the character, and distribution of the population, and the temper of Russia and other powers by whom it would have to be established and maintained.

The only other method is radical and vigorous administrative reforms, which the European powers should initiate, and report to Turkey, instead of *vice versa*, as arranged in Article LXI. of the Berlin Treaty. These "Christian nations" have for sixteen years violated most sacred treaty obligations, and England a special guarantee for such reforms. While attended with difficulties, this is the most desirable solution, and is favored by the great mass of Armenians throughout Turkey, by the Anglo-Armenian Association,[1] founded by Prof. James Bryce, M.P., and by the Phil-Armenic Society in this country.[2] The real spirit and aim of the Armenian race, as a whole, is unfortunately obscured, in the mind of the public, by utterances and acts of a few irresponsible Armenian hot-heads, who have imbibed nihilistic views in Europe, and are trying, in a very bungling way, to apply them.

[1] *The Case for the Armenians.* London: Anglo-Armenian Association.

[2] *An Appeal to the Christians of America by the Christians of Armenia.* New York: Phil-Armenic Society.

CHAPTER IV.

OTTOMAN PROMISES AND THEIR FULFILMENT.

IMPERIAL edicts of toleration, and promises of reform on the part of the Sublime Porte, have been very numerous, and have served Turkey well as political expedients. Their value is that of so much dust thrown in the eyes of Europe when her aid or her mercy was needful. As these reforms have all been promised under pressure, they have likewise been abandoned just so fast and so far as the pressure has been removed. In many cases there has been serious retrogression. The sow that is washed is forever returning to wallow in the mire. It is as true of the "Sick Man" as of him out of whom seven devils were cast, that the last state of that man is worse than the first. This is emphatically so in regard to the freedom of the press, the curtailment of religious and educational privileges, and the safety of the lives and property of Christians.

The following is a partial list of Turkish promises which have been broken in whole or in part, with the circumstances under which they were made.

1. In 1829, by the Treaty of Adrianople at the close of a war with Russia, Turkey promised to re-

form in her treatment of Orthodox Christians, and acknowledged Russia's right to interfere in their behalf.[1]

2. In 1839 Sultan Abd-ul-Medjid, in order to enlist European sympathy and aid—when the victorious Egyptian army under Ibrahim Pasha was threatening Constantinople—issued an Imperial rescript, the Hatti Sherif, in which he promised to protect the life, honor, and property of all his subjects irrespective of race or religion.

3. In 1844 the same Sultan Abd-ul-Medjid gave a solemn pledge that thenceforth no apostate from Mohammedanism *who had formerly been a Christian* should be put to death. This pledge was extorted from the Sultan by the Ambassador of Great Britain, supported by those of other Powers, after the public execution in Constantinople of a young Armenian, Ovagim, who had declared himself a Mohammedan, but who afterwards bravely maintained his Christian profession in the face of torture and death. Since that time many Moslems even have embraced Christianity, and have been put out of the way, quietly in most cases.

4. In 1850 the same Sultan, on the demand of the same Powers, in view of the continued and fierce persecution of the Protestant subjects of the Porte, granted the latter a charter, guaranteeing them liberty of conscience and all the rights as a distinct civil community, which had been enjoyed by the other Christian communities of the empire. But to this day the numerous Protestants of Stamboul have

[1] Morfill's *Russia*, p. 287. Putnam.

never been allowed to erect even *one church*, although they have owned a site and had the necessary funds, and been petitioning for a firman to build for fifteen years.¹ The Greek Protestants of Ordoo, who have a church, are not allowed to worship in it. There are many other flagrant violations of this charter.

5. In 1856, after the Crimean War, Sultan Abd-ul-Medjid, to anticipate demands which he knew would be included in the Treaty of Paris then being drawn up, issued the Imperial edict known as the Hatti Humayoun. This edict not only promised perfect equality of civil rights to all subjects of the Porte, but also added: "As all forms of religion are and shall be freely professed in my dominions, no subject of my empire shall be hindered in the exercise of the religion that he professes, nor shall he in any way be annoyed on this account." But as the interpretation and enforcement of this edict has remained absolutely in the hands of the Turkish Government, it is needless to add that it has been a dead letter.²

6. In 1878 the Anglo-Turkish Convention, entered into just before the Treaty of Berlin, included these

¹ Rev. H. O. Dwight, *The Independent*, New York, January 17, 1895.
² At the time of the Crimean War Lord Aberdeen said:

"Notwithstanding the favorable opinion entertained by many, it is difficult to believe in the improvement of the Turks. It is true that, under the pressure of the moment, benevolent decrees may be issued; but these, except under the eye of some Foreign Minister, are entirely neglected. Their whole system is radically vicious and inhuman. I do not refer to fables which may be invented at St. Petersburg or Vienna, but to numerous despatches of Lord Stratford (de Radcliffe) himself, and of our own consuls, who describe a frightful picture of lawless oppression and cruelty." (Sir Theodore Martin's *Life of the Prince Consort*, vol. ii., p. 528.) Quoted by Canon MacColl, *The Contemporary Review*, January, 1895.

words in its First Article: "His Imperial Majesty, the Sultan, promises to England to introduce necessary reforms, to be agreed upon later between the two Powers, into the government and for the protection of the Christian and other subjects of the Porte in these territories [Armenia]; and in order to enable England to make necessary provision for executing her engagement [the keeping of Russia out of Armenia], His Imperial Majesty, the Sultan, further consents to assign the Island of Cyprus to be occupied and administered by England." Comment unnecessary.

7. In July, 1878, by the Treaty of Berlin, religious liberty and the public exercise of all forms of religion were guaranteed in separate articles to the people of Bulgaria, Eastern Roumelia, Montenegro, Servia, Roumania, and finally to all subjects of the Porte in every part of the Ottoman Empire. Cases of glaring violation of the principle of religious liberty may be found in Appendix C. on *The Censorship of the Press.*

The Sixty-first Article of the same treaty reads thus: "The Sublime Porte undertakes to carry out, without further delay, the improvements and reforms demanded by local requirements in the provinces inhabited by the Armenians, and to guarantee their security against the Circassians and Kurds. It will periodically make known the steps taken to this effect to the Powers, who will superintend their application."

What the condition of Turkey was three years later, not simply in Armenia, but throughout Asia Minor, is shown by a report of Mr. Wilson, British Consul-General in Anatolia.

"There has probably never been a time in which

the prestige of the Courts has fallen so low, or in which the administration of justice has been so venal and corrupt. The most open and shameless bribery is practised from highest to lowest; prompt, even-handed justice for rich and poor alike is unknown; sentence is given in favor of the suitor who 'places' his money most judiciously; imprisonment or freedom has in many places become a matter of bribery; robbers, when arrested, are protected by members of the Court, who share their spoil; a simple order may send an innocent man to prison for months; crime goes unpunished, and all manner of oppression and injustice is committed with impunity. The Cadis,[1] especially those in the cazas,[2] are, as a rule, ignorant men, with no education, knowing little of law, except the Sheri, on which they base their decisions, and sometimes not overmuch of that. As to the members, it is sufficient to say that they are nearly all equally ignorant of law, and that probably not twenty-five per cent. of them can write Turkish, or read the sentences to which they attach their seals. In the Commercial Courts, the Presidents are frequently entirely ignorant of the duties which they have to perform. The low pay of the Cadis, the short term —two years—during which they hold their appointments, and the manner in which they obtain them, render the receipt of bribes almost a necessity. The first thought of a Cadi who buys an appointment in the provinces is to recoup himself for his outlay; the second, to obtain enough money to purchase a new place when his term of office is finished. Even under this system men are to be found who refuse

[1] Judge.   [2] Local districts.

to receive bribes; and there are others who, whilst giving way to temptation, deplore the necessity to do so."[1]

The sequel to the Treaty of Berlin is found in the next chapter.

The non-fulfilment of Ottoman promises in regard to Christian subjects, and the frequent massacres of the latter are an exact fulfilment of

THE OFFICIAL PRAYER OF ISLAM

which is used throughout Turkey, and daily repeated in the Cairo "Azhar" University by ten thousand Mohammedan students from all lands. The following translation is from the Arabic:

"I seek refuge with Allah from Satan, [the *rejeem*] the accursed. In the name of Allah the Compassionate, the Merciful! O Lord of all Creatures! O Allah! Destroy the infidels and polytheists, thine enemies, the enemies of the religion! O Allah! Make their children orphans, and defile their abodes! Cause their feet to slip; give them and their families, their households and their women, their children and their relations by marriage, their brothers and their friends, their possessions and their race, their wealth and their lands, as booty to the Moslems, O Lord of all Creatures!"[2]

All who do not accept Mohammed are included among "the infidels" referred to in the prayer.

[1] Report of Mr. Wilson, *Blue-Book*, Turkey, No. 8 (1880), page 57, No. 48.
[2] *The Mohammedan Missionary Problem*, p. 31. Jessup, Philadelphia, Presb. Pub. Soc.

CHAPTER V.

THE OUTCOME OF THE TREATY OF BERLIN.

IT is quite needless to remark that Turkey, instead of doing anything to improve the condition of the Armenians, has done much to make it worse during the past fifteen years. The question now arises, what have the Powers signatory to the Berlin Treaty done to compel the Sublime Porte "to carry out the improvements and reforms" demanded in the Sixty-first Article? And what steps has Great Britain taken in addition, to discharge the additional obligation for the improvement of Armenia which she assumed by the so-called Cyprus Convention?

We find that in November, 1879, the English Government, seeing that matters throughout Asia Minor were really going from bad to worse, went the length of ordering an English squadron to the Archipelago for the purpose of a naval demonstration. The Turkish Government was greatly excited, and with a view to getting the order countermanded, made the fairest promises.

But England was not the only Power aroused. On June 11, 1880, an Identical Note of the Great Powers demanded the execution of the clauses of the Treaty of Berlin which had remained in suspense. In the conclusion of the Identical Note a clear recognition is made of the fact that *the interest of Europe, as well as that of the Ottoman Empire, requires the execution of the Sixty-first Article of the Treaty of Berlin, and that the joint and incessant action of the Powers can alone bring about this result.*

On July 5th, the Turkish Foreign Minister sent a Note in reply to the representatives of the Powers. " It is of great length and small real value, except as combining in a remarkable degree the distinguishing characteristics of modern Ottoman diplomacy, namely, first, great facility in assimilating the administrative and constitutional jargon of civilized countries; second, consummate cunning in concealing under deceptive appearances the barbarous reality of deeds and intentions; third, cool audacity in making promises which there is neither the power nor desire to make good; and, finally, a paternal and oily tone, intended to create the impression that the Turkish Government is the victim of unjust prejudices and odious calumnies."

As soon as the reply of the Porte was received, Earl Granville sent copies to the British Consuls in Asia Minor, inviting observations thereon. Eight detailed replies to this request are published in the Blue-Book.[1] They concur in a crushing condemnation of the Ottoman Government.

These conclusions, moderately and very diffusely expressed in diplomatic phraseology, are reflected in

[1] *Blue-Book*, Turkey, No. 6, 1881, reports of Wilson, Bennett, Chermside, Trotter, Stewart, Clayton, Everett, and Bilotti.

the Collective Note which was sent on Sept. 11, 1880, to the Sublime Porte by the Ambassadors of the Great Powers. On October 3d, without making the slightest references to censures which had been addressed to it, and even appearing completely to ignore the Collective Note, the Porte, assuming a haughty tone, merely notified the Powers of what it intended to do.

In a Circular of the 12th of January, 1881, Earl Granville tried again to induce the other five Powers to join in further representations to the Sublime Porte on the subject. But the other Powers seem to have thought that the diplomatic comedy had gone far enough, and sent evasive answers. Prince Bismarck expressed the opinion that there would be "serious inconvenience" in raising the Armenian question, and France hid behind Germany. Such action by the powers had been anticipated by the British Ambassador at Constantinople, Mr. Goschen, who had already written to Earl Granville: "If they [the Powers] refuse, or give only lukewarm support, the responsibility will not lie with Her Majesty's Government." The whole correspondence was simply a matter of form.[1] I have condensed this outline of events since the Treaty of Berlin from *Armenia, the Armenians, and the Treaties*,[2] following as far as possible the words of the writer, M. G. Rolin-Jacquemyns, a high authority on International Law.

From 1881 to the present time, almost without exception, England, on her part, has allowed

---

[1] *Blue-Book*, Turkey, 1881, p. 242.
[2] Published by John Heywood, London, 1891, pp. 82–89.

no mention in her Blue-Books of the manner in which her *protégés* and those of Europe have been treated. Her energies have seemed to be devoted to stifling the ever-increasing cry of despair from Armenia, instead of attempting her rescue or relief. The other Powers are only less guilty, in proportion as they have done less to perpetuate Ottoman misrule, and have made less pretence of sympathy and help for the oppressed. Freeman says of England,

"By waging a war on behalf of the Turk, by signing a treaty which left the nations of South-eastern Europe [and Asia Minor] at the mercy of the Turk, by propping up the wicked power of the Turk in many ways, we have done a great wrong to the nations which are under his yoke; and that wrong which we have ourselves done it is our duty to undo."[1]

It is thus clearly seen that both the Sixty-first Article of the Berlin Treaty, and the Cyprus Convention as well, have been of positively no value in securing for the Armenians any of the reforms which were therein recognized as imperatively called for and guaranteed. It is also clear that the condition of Armenia, and of Turkey as a whole, is even vastly worse and more hopeless than it was twenty years ago.

This condition, I further maintain, is in large measure directly attributable to those treaties themselves and to the attitude subsequently assumed by the Powers which signed them. It is said that the Armenians have brought trouble on themselves, by stirring up the Turks. I ask what stirred the Armenians up? It was primarily the Sixty-first Article

[1] Freeman, *The Turks in Europe*.

of the Treaty of Berlin. Many a time has that precious paragraph been quoted to me in the wilds of Kurdistan by common Armenian artisans and

PROFESSOR MINAS TCHÉRAZ.
Present at the Berlin Congress.

ignorant villagers. They had welcomed it as a second evangel, and believed the word of England as they did the gospels. *It was that Article which* roused them from the torpor of centuries. They saw Bulgaria rise from her blood and shame and enter on a career of honor and prosperity under the ægis of European protection. Is it surprising that hopes and aspirations have been born anew in the heart of the Armenian race—a people not inferior to the Bulgarians and in many respects more talented?

I have rarely found it difficult to persuade intelligent Armenians that an autonomous Armenia is impracticable. But I have never been able to convince one of them that the course of England and the other powers has been anything but one of selfishness, jealousy, and dishonor as far as fulfilment of their treaty obligations is concerned.

During a residence of four years in Eastern Turkey I noticed a marked and rapid alienation of Armenian sentiment from England in favor of Russia, who now seems to them the only source of succor. *They see in England only a dog in the manger.*

There is another sequel to the Berlin Treaty and to the attitude of the powers, namely, its effect on the Turks themselves. The natural enmity and contempt of the Moslem rulers and population generally for the Christian subjects has been greatly increased by reason of the pressure which foreign Powers have occasionally brought to bear on the Turks in order to procure relief for the Christian. To be sure the only hope of such relief is from without. But the pressure should not be of a petty, nagging and galling nature. This is worse than nothing. *What is needed is prompt, decisive, and final action.*

And things have now arrived at such a pass that in such action lies the only hope of preventing a terrible catastrophe, which will eclipse even the massacres of Sassoun. The wheels of progress will not go backward except as they are broken. The Christians of Armenia can be exterminated, but it is too late for them to accept slavery or Islam. They may be slaughtered like sheep, but they will not all die like dogs. The revolutionary movement, as it is called, is thus far nothing but a blind turning of the worm. It is ill considered, without resources, reckless, and foreign to the real spirit, objects, and methods of the Armenians on Turkish soil. It is not denied that there are a few Armenians in Europe who, in despair and for lack of better teaching, have imbibed Nihilistic views and are trying, in a very bungling way, to apply them. They are hated by the vast majority of Armenians in Turkey. They are related to the question at issue in the same way and degree as train wreckers and box-car burners were to the industrial problem during the riots of Chicago in July last, and deserve the same treatment. The Turks take great pains to thrust them into public notice, as a cloak for themselves, and with good success. The Turkish Government and its partisans, in order to conceal the real character of the massacre in Sassoun, have made persistent, extensive, and dishonorable use of a letter by the first President of Robert College, Constantinople, Dr. Cyrus Hamlin, written December 23, 1894. Dr. Hamlin's vigorous and indignant protest may be found in Appendix C.

The idea of Armenian revolution is a new thing

in the history of that peaceable race, which has quietly submitted for centuries to the yoke of the Turk. But it is the natural outcome of the horrible situation in Armenia since the Treaty of Berlin, and the disease is bound to grow more virulent and contagious until the European doctors apply vigorous and radical treatment to the "Sick Man." It is difficult to see how anything but a surgical operation can be helpful. The knife has frequently been used in the case of this incurable patient during the present century, and always with excellent results, as for instance in the case of Greece, Lebanon, Bulgaria, Boznia-Herzegovina, and Egypt.

ZEIBEK, TURKISH SOLDIER, "IRREGULAR."

A situation in many respects parallel to that in Armenia existed until lately in Bosnia and Herzegovina. How quickly and completely that difficult problem has been solved, is narrated by M. de Blowitz in the October,

1894, issue of *The Nineteenth Century*, from which I condense in his own words.

"The orders, given after the taking over of the country, to surrender all arms or to destroy them, was given a sweeping application. Yet, before the victorious entry of the Austro-Hungarians, each Bosnian each Herzegovinian, was a walking arsenal.

"To-day weapons and ambuscades are things of the romantic past. Twelve years have sufficed, under M. de Kallay's administration, not only to remove all traces of the wild, inhospitable, inaccessible Bosnia of which I have been speaking, but indeed and especially to banish even the memory of those dark days of strenuous battle, and to wipe away from the hearts of both invader and invaded all traces of the hate which then animated them. In the year 1882, the superior administration of the two provinces (Bosnia and Herzegovina) passed into the hands of the Minister of Finance of the Austro-Hungarian Empire, who was then, and who is still, M. de Kallay. From this moment all is changed. The powers given to the new administration are almost unlimited. The civil element has been substituted for the military element, and pacification has succeeded conquest. The greatest effort is made to reassure all minds. Not a single minaret has disappeared, not a *muezzin* is deprived of his resources."

A recent writer wisely says that "the Armenian question, if it ever be settled at all, must be taken out of the Turk's hands, whether he like it or not. . . . And we have an opportunity now, which may never come our way again, of settling a difficulty which, if allowed to develop much longer, will prove more fruitful of mischief than any with which we have been confronted for a generation or more."[1]

C. B. Norman, special correspondent of *The London Times*, in his *Armenia and the Campaign of 1877*[2] wrote words which are even truer to-day. I condense:

"Naturally, since I have been here I have had many, very many, opportunities of conversing with Turkish officers and men on the so-called Eastern Question; and the consequence is that, arriving in the country a strong philo-Turk, deeply impressed with the necessity of preserving the 'integrity of the Empire' in order to uphold 'British interests,' I now fain would cry with Mr. Freeman: 'Perish, British interests, perish our dominion in India, rather than that we should strike a blow on behalf of the wrong against the right!'"[3]

"There is no finer race in the world than the Turk

TURKISH SOLDIER, "REGULAR."

---

[1] "Diplomatist," "The Armenian Question" in *The New Review*, January, 1895.
[2] Pp. 158-9. London: Cassell, Petter, & Galpin.
[3] Speech in St. James's Hall, December, 1876.

proper. Brave, honest, industrious, truthful, frugal, kind-hearted, and hospitable, all who *know* the Osmanli speak well of him. He is as much oppressed by the curse of misgovernment as his Christian fellow-subject; and had the members of the Eastern Question Association as keen a sense of justice as they have love of writing, they would long ago have obliterated the word 'Christian' from their lengthy documents, and striven to ameliorate the condition of the lower orders of the subjects of the Porte, downtrodden as they are by an effete section of the Mohammedan race, who have degenerated in mind, body, and estate, since coming in contact with Western civilization.

"I do not for one moment mean to deny that there are honest, energetic Turks, capable of exercising their talents for their country's good; but these men are powerless. The vital powers of the nation are so sapped by centuries of misrule, the minds of the majority are so imbued with the belief that all ideas not born of Moslem brains and sanctified by Moslem usage are false, and to be scorned, that were any honest-minded gentleman to rise to power, and endeavor to check the present system of misgovernment, he would not remain in office one week. Captain Gambier's able article on the 'Life of Midhat Pasha'[1] bears me out in this idea."

[1] *The Nineteenth Century*, January, 1878.

CHAPTER VI.

THE SULTAN AND THE SUBLIME PORTE.

CHURCH and State are one and inseparable in Turkey. The Sultan of the empire is also Calif of the Mohammedan religious world. He cannot abdicate either office, if he would, without vacating the other by the same act. In fact, herein lies the secret of the present Sultan's policy, which seems suicidal on general principles of government. He has, on the one hand, been lavish in the building and repairing of mosques, and in establishing Moslem schools throughout his dominions. On the other hand, he has infringed and ignored the ancient rights and privileges of the Christian Patriarchates which were guaranteed by Mohammed II., and have hitherto been regarded as sacred. He has blocked the erection of new Christian schools and churches, and even the repairing of such as are falling into decay. There were formerly thousands of non-Moslems in civil positions, faithfully serving the government; under the new régime, however, they have been systematically removed and excluded. And why has all this been done? Because the Sultan is a good conscientious Mohammedan, it is only fair to believe. Even if he were not a sincere believer, he would still feel compelled to adopt the same course, as a matter of internal political necessity. The Moslem population look to him as the Defender of the Faith, girded with the sword of the Prophet. He feels it imperative at all hazards to regain lost prestige over his fanatical subjects, especially in the south, where rumblings of discontent and disloyalty are ominous.[1]

Let us be reasonable and practical. Why longer exact or accept from the Sultan promises which he cannot make without doing violence to his own conscience and to his office, and which he cannot execute without imperilling his throne? You might as well ask the Pope to abandon the doctrines of temporal sovereignty and of infallibility, which to him are fundamental. If the situation in Turkey demands that anything be done, and if the rest of humanity and civilization have any responsibility in the matter, let practical statesmen proceed to business. All hope of reform from within depends on

---

[1] From a descendant of Dahir Billah, the thirty-fifth caliph of Bagdad, Sultan Selim I. "procured the cession of his claims, and obtained the right to deem himself the shadow of God upon earth. Since then the Ottoman padishah has been held to inherit the rights of Omar and Haroun, and to be the legitimate commander of the faithful, and, as such, possessed of plenary temporal and spiritual authority over the followers of Mohammed."[2] The Persians and Moors, however, reject this claim, and at the close of the Russian War not a few of the Arab muftis declared that the caliphate had been forfeited by the inglorious defeat of the Turks, and should now return to the Arab family of Koreish.

[2] Freeman, *The Saracens*, p. 158. Quoted by Jessup, *The Mohammedan Missionary Problem*, p. 21. Philadelphia: Presbyterian Board of Publication, 1879.

the distrustful, distracted, hoodwinked Sultan, who is clearly, in the circumstances, a helpless and pitiable object. But he should no more be allowed to stand in the way of the emancipation of Turkey, than the Pope was allowed to impede the making of Italy. "The Prisoner of the Vatican" has still abundant scope for his great and beneficent spiritual projects; and the Captive at Yildiz Palace—for such he has for years constituted himself—may also be allowed a sphere in which his personal virtues and ability shall shine forth, unobscured by the clouds and darkness that surround him now. He certainly would be better off, and his subjects also—Moslem no less than Christian.

The shrieks of ten thousand slaughtered Armenians pierce for the moment above the groans of others. But it should not be forgotten that all the races in Turkey are under the same curse, and that the present is a chance to help them as well as the Armenians.

According to the Koran, which is the basis and ultimate authority of Mohammedan law—Code Napoleon, treaty stipulations, and Imperial *Iradés* notwithstanding,—the whole non-Moslem population of Turkey are outlaws. The millions of ancient, hereditary inhabitants, whether Greek, Armenian, Nestorian, Jacobite, Jew, or Syrian, are considered aliens. Their legal status is that of prisoners of war, with corresponding rights and responsibilities.' Not one of them is expected or even allowed to serve in the army. Non-Moslems, whose services are indis-

[1] Hughes, *Notes on Muhammadanism*, pp. 209, 210.

pensable to the government, are, in rare cases, put in civil offices, especially financial, for which no Mohammedan of sufficient integrity or ability can be found.

It cannot be denied that the above is true in theory, and it is equally true that the theory is carried out so far as fear of intervention by Christian nations permits.

But in this hour, when our hearts are stirred by the lot of our co-religionists under the Crescent, let us not forget that the Moslem population almost equally is cursed and impoverished by Turkish misrule, venality, and taxation. They drink the cup of woe, all but the more bitter dregs of religious persecution, which is reserved for Christian lips. Their benumbed condition, natural stolidity, and unquestioning obedience to Islam, a creed whose cardinal principle is submission,[1] accounts for the fact that they do not appear as a factor of the problem. Yet even Mohammedans often secretly come pleading that Europe take some interest in their case too. In the name of humanity, yes, of Christianity, let them not be forgotten.

"An Eastern Resident," writing from Constantinople, in an article entitled " Sultan Abd-ul-Hamid," in *The Contemporary Review*, January, 1895, gives an able analysis of the Sultan's position and policy, showing at the same time great appreciation of His Majesty as a man. His position and relations to the Sublime Porte are not well understood by the public, and could hardly be better stated than in these extracts:

[1] Hughes, *Notes on Muhammadanism*, p. 10.

The Sultan and the Sublime Porte. 91

"So far as we can judge, the Sultan is a sincere and honest Mohammedan, and regards himself as a

H. I. M. ABD-UL-HAMID KHAN, THE SULTAN OF TURKEY.

true Caliph—a successor of the Prophet—the chief defender of the faith, under God the absolute arbiter of its destinies. He has undoubtedly done his best to reconcile the interests of the Caliphate with those of the Empire. . . .

" In one particular it [the policy of the Sultan] is condemned by most enlightened Mohammedans as strongly as by Christians. His attempt to concentrate the whole administration of the Empire in his own hands has led to the establishment of a dual government—that of the Palace and the Porte. The whole machinery of a government exists at the Porte. There are Ministers and fully organized departments. There is a Council of Ministers and a Council of State. All business is supposed to pass through their hands, and the whole administration is supposed to be subordinate to them. All is, of course, subject to the supreme will of the Sultan, but his official advisers and his official agents are at the Porte.

" In fact, however, there is another government at the Palace of Yildiz, more powerful than the official government, made up of chamberlains, mollahs, eunuchs, astrologers, and nondescripts, and supported by the secret police, which spares no one from the Grand Vizier down. The general policy of the Empire is determined by this government, and the most important questions of state are often treated and decided, while the highest officials of the Porte are left in absolute ignorance of what is going on. It is needless to add that the Porte and the Palace are at sword's-point, and block each other's movements as far as they can. . . .

" The Sultan evidently believes that he is equally independent of both these governments, and decides all questions, great and small, for himself. In form he does so, but no man can act independently of all his sources of information, and of the personal influence of his *entourage*. Under the present system he makes himself responsible for every blunder and every iniquity committed in the Empire, but he has disgraced three distinguished Grand Viziers for telling him so, and seems to have no idea of the causes of the intense dissatisfaction with his government which prevails among his Mohammedan subjects. The Turks, as well as the Christians, also condemn the laws restricting personal freedom, which have increased in severity every year. In many ways these laws are more galling to the Turks than the Christians. . . .

" There is another evil connected with this system which may lead to serious difficulties with foreign Powers. All foreign relations are supposed to be managed through the Minister of Foreign Affairs or the Grand Vizier, but these officials have no power and but little influence. They can promise nothing and do nothing. But in all delicate diplomatic questions it is essential to treat with responsible agents, and to discuss them with such agents in a way in which it is impossible to treat with the Sovereign himself. The present system has been a serious injury to Turkey. It has roused the hostility of all the Embassies and led them to feel and report to their governments, that there is no use in trying to do anything to save this Empire; that it is hopelessly corrupt, and the sooner it comes to an end the better for the world. There is no longer any concerted action of Europe at Constantinople for the improvement of the condition of the people. . . .

"If Sultan Abd-ul-Hamid would come out of his palace, restore to the Porte its full responsibility, disband its secret police, trust his Mohammedan subjects, and do simple justice to the Christians, his life would be far more secure than it is to-day, with all precautions; his people and all the world would recognize the great and noble qualities which they now ignore, and welcome him as the wisest and best of all the Sultans. . . .

"The sad pity of it is that he will never do it. It is too late. The influence of the Palace favorites is too strong. He will appear in history not as the Sultan who saved the Empire, but as the one who might have saved it and did not."

CHAPTER VII.

PREVIOUS ACTS OF THE TURKISH TRAGEDY.

IN this chapter[1] I shall take no account of events that have taken place in legitimate warfare, where the slain were foreign enemies or rebellious subjects of the Sultan, resisting with arms in their hands after being ordered to submit. The "insurgents"—as the Porte has called them—in all these cases have consisted of men, women, children, and infants, and in each case, by a curious coincidence, have been non-Mohammedan.

In all of these massacres, Turkish military or civil officers presided and directed the bloody work, as will be seen by reference to the authorities mentioned. There have been many other massacres of less than ten thousand during the intervals, which, to use the language of Beder Khan in Mosul (see Layard's *Nineveh*), have confirmed the whole Turkish principle, that "the Armenians were becoming too numerous, and needed diminishing."

---

[1] Parts of this chapter are taken from an article, "Notes on the Armenian Massacre," in *The Independent*, New York, January 31, 1895, by a high authority, who is compelled to sign himself "A Student of Modern History."

This item of Turkey's account, for the past seventy-five years only, stands about as follows:

DEFENSELESS CHRISTIAN SUBJECTS MASSACRED IN TURKEY 1820 TO 1894.

1822. Greeks, especially in Scio (Chios)	50,000[1]
1850. Nestorians and Armenians, Kurdistan	10,000[2]
1860. Maronites and Syrians, Lebanon and Damascus	11,000[3]
1876. Bulgarians, Bulgaria	10,000[4]
1894. Armenians, Armenia, Sassoun	12,000[5]
Total	93,000

The above figures indicate the extent of the massacres mentioned. The following extracts reveal the occasion and manner in which they were carried out.

The first extract is in regard to the Greeks, and is a translation, by Mr. Robert Stein, from the French:

"The blow had been long premeditated. Sultan Mahmoud was in the habit of replying to every success of the Greek insurgents by ordering massacres,

---

[1] Latham, *Russian and Turk*, p. 417. London: W. H. Allen, 1878.

[2] Layard's *Nineveh*.

[3] Colonel Churchill, *Druses and Maronites*, p. 219. London: Quaritch, 1862.

[4] Eugene Schuyler and Correspondent MacGahan, quoted in *The Independent*, January 10, 1895.

[5] Chapter I. of this book.

violations, and enslavement in regions without defense, where there were none but women, children, and inoffensive merchants. After the first exploit of Kanaris, the quiet commercial town of Cydonia had promptly been burnt. The Turkish admiral was beaten at Samos; for that reason thirty days were spent in Cyprus in cutting off heads. The town of Tripolitza, in the Morea, having been taken by the Palikares, the inhabitants of Cassandra, in Thrace, were given up to bands of Arnauts. The Sultan wished to take new reprisals to terrify the *rayas* [Christian subjects], and to cause the nations of Europe to reflect. He took care not to fix his choice on Crete, where his *nizams* would have been received with gunshots. Chios was an easy prey, and suspected nothing, having always lived on good terms with the Porte, and having even refused to take part in the insurrection of Hellas and the islands. The Chiotes had always been the gentlest, the most docile, the most timid of all the *rayas*. The secret societies which endeavored to rouse the Greek people had not even deigned to initiate these islanders in their projects of national resurrection. On the 8th of May, 1821, the intrepid Tombasis, with fifteen brigs from Hydra and ten schooners from Psara, had appeared before the island, and his patriotic advances having been ill received, he had retired. The inhabitants of Chios, in order to give new guaranties of submission, had sent to the Turks large amounts of money, numerous hostages, and all their arms; even the little knives with which they cut their bread had been taken from them.

"At this moment, on Easter Day, 1822, the Capitan-Pasha anchored in the harbor, with seven ships and eight frigates. Inasmuch as many of the people, frightened by the sight of this fleet, had fled to the mountains, they were made to come down by promises of safety, and by sending to them some consuls, who were simple enough to lend themselves in good faith to this ignoble fraud. The Turkish admiral brought his executioners with him; *bashi-bazouks* from Rumelia, Zeibeks and Yuruks from Asia Minor, the most ferocious and cowardly to be found in the empire. The adventurers had come in great numbers, eager for their prey, attracted by this country, so rich in harvests, in gold coins, and in women. On the day fixed for this surprise all this rabble was crowded into boats, with pistols and knives, and the carnage began. Whole regiments courageously besieged villages containing three hundred souls. For many of them, this slaughter was a great joke, a gigantic *bakshish*. They slashed and burned all day; in the evening they reckoned up the price of the slaves, the sheep, the goats, all huddled together pell-mell in the profaned churches. The children and the women escaped death; their youth and beauty saved them from the massacre, to deliver them over at once to outrageous assaults or to reserve them for the shameful fate of the harem. They were led off in long troops; they were put on the market and sold in the bazaars of Smyrna, Constantinople, and Brussa. Whatever resisted was killed without mercy. At Mesta, a young girl cried and struggled against an Arnaut; the madman seized her loosened hair, turned back the collar, and with a cut of his sabre severed the pretty head. The person who described this scene to me saw it with his own eyes."[1]

In regard to the massacre of Nestorians in 1850, Layard states that after 9000 had been massacred, "1000 men, women, and children concealed themselves in a mountain fastness. Beder Khan Beg, an officer of rank in the employment of the Sultan, unable to get at them, surrounded the place, and waited until they should be compelled to yield by thirst and hunger. Then he offered to spare their lives on the surrender of their arms and property, terms ratified by an oath on the Koran. The Kurds were then admitted to the platform. After they had disarmed their prisoners they commenced an indiscriminate slaughter, until, weary of using their weapons, they hurled the few survivors from the rocks into the river Zab below. Out of nearly 1000 only one escaped."[2]

In regard to the massacre of Maronites and Syrians in 1860, the anonymous authority in *The Independent* goes on to say:

"After the massacre of June and July, 1860, in Lebanon and Damascus, under the direction of Tahir Pasha in Deir el Komr, Osman Beg in Hasbeiya, Kurshid Pasha in Lebanon, and Ahmed Pasha in Damascus, a conference was held in Paris, August 3d, by the representatives of Great Britain, Austria, France, Prussia, Russia, and Turkey. As 11,000

---

[1] M. Gaston Deschamps: "En Turquie—L'Ile de Chio," *Revue des Deux Mondes*, p. 167, January 1, 1893.

[2] Layard's *Nineveh*, pp. 24-201.

Christians had been massacred, the European representatives called the attention of the Sultan to his promise in the Treaty of Paris, March 30, 1856, 'that serious administrative measures should be taken to ameliorate the condition of the Christian population of every sect in the Ottoman Empire.' . . . And then, in the presence and with the consent of the five aforesaid Christian representatives, assembled together for the express purpose of taking measures to stop the effusion of Christian blood in Syria, caused by the wicked and wilful collusion of the Sultan's authorities, the following insult to the common sense, the feelings, and judgment of Christian Europe was deliberately penned: 'The Plenipotentiary of the Sublime Porte takes note of this declaration of the representatives of the high contracting Powers, and undertakes to transmit it to his court, pointing out *that the Sublime Porte has employed, and continues to employ, her efforts in the sense of the wish expressed above!*' " (Churchill, pp. 220, 221.)

Colonel Churchill further says (p. 222):

"Nejib Pasha, who was installed Governor of the Pashalick of Damascus on the restoration of Syria to the Sultan in 1840, declared to a confidential agent of the British Consul in that city, not knowing, however, the character of the person he was addressing, 'the Turkish Government can only maintain its supremacy in Syria by cutting down the Christian sects.' What Nejib Pasha enounced as a theory, Kurshid Pasha, after an interval of twenty years, succeeded in carrying into practice."

The writer in *The Independent* adds:

"Thus we have Nejib Pasha in 1840, Beder Khan in 1850, Kurshid Pasha in 1860, Chefket Pasha in 1876, and Zekki Pasha in 1894, concurring in this noble and philanthropic scheme for relieving the Turkish Empire of its surplus Christian population!"

The following facts relate to the terrible atrocities perpetrated in Bulgaria by Turkish *bashi-bazouks* in the spring of 1876. I quote verbatim from the preliminary report[1] of the Hon. Eugene Schuyler, American Consul-General, to the Hon. Horace Maynard, the American Minister, at Constantinople:

"PHILIPPOPOLIS, August 10, 1876.

"SIR:—In reference to the atrocities and massacres committed by the Turks in Bulgaria, I have the honor to inform you that I have visited the towns of Adrianople, Philippopolis, and Tatar-Bazardjik, and villages in the surrounding districts. From what I have personally seen, and from the inquiries I have made, and the information I have received, I have ascertained the following facts: . . .

"The insurgent villages made little or no resistance. In many instances they surrendered their arms upon the first demand. Nearly all the villages which were attacked by the *bashi-bazouks* were burned and pillaged, as were also all those which had been abandoned by the terrified inhabitants. The inhabitants of some villages were massacred after exhibitions of the most ferocious cruelty, and the violation not only of women and girls, but even of persons of the other sex. These crimes were

---

[1] Article by Mr. Savage, *The Independent*, January 10, 1894.

committed by the regular troops as well as by the *bashi-bazouks* [irregulars]. The number of villages which were burned in whole or in part in the districts of Philippopolis, Roptchus, and Tatar-Bazardjik is at least sixty-five.

"Particular attention was given by the troops to the churches and schools, which in some cases were destroyed with petroleum and gunpowder.

"It is difficult to estimate the number of Bulgarians who were killed during the few days that the disturbances lasted; but I am inclined to put 15,000 as the lowest for the districts I have named. . . . This village surrendered, without firing a shot, after a promise of safety, to the *bashi-bazouks*, under command of Ahmed Aga, a chief of the rural police. Despite his promise, the arms once surrendered, Ahmed Aga ordered the destruction of the village and the indiscriminate slaughter of the inhabitants, about a hundred young girls being reserved to satisfy the lust of the conqueror before they too should be killed. Not a house is now standing in this lovely valley. Of the 8000 inhabitants not 2000 are known to survive.

"Ahmed Aga, who commanded the massacre, has since been decorated and promoted to the rank of *yuz bashi* [centurian].

"These atrocities were clearly unnecessary for the suppression of the insurrection, for it was an insignificant rebellion at the best, and the villagers generally surrendered at the first summons.

"I am, sir, yours very truly,

"EUGENE SCHUYLER.

"The Hon. HORACE MAYNARD, etc."

"The British Government had glossed over and tried to cover up these horrible transactions, Premier Disraeli turning them off with a sneer. The facts, as unearthed by Consul Schuyler, shook the British nation like an earthquake, and came near unseating the Ministry. . . .

"A similar investigation was made in the same district by Mr. J. A. MacGahan, the brilliant correspondent of the London *Daily News*, who confirms all that Mr. Schuyler discovered, in a special despatch to the *Daily News*, dated Philippopolis, July 28, 1876."

The circumstances and character of the Armenian massacre of 1894 are found in the first chapter of the present volume. In regard to this event the writer in *The Independent* of January 17th above quoted asks:

"Will history repeat itself in 1895? Will the remaining Armenians of Sassoun be so terrorized as to refuse to testify before a Commission? Undoubtedly.

"If the facts already known do not force Europe to place Eastern Asia Minor under a Christian Viceroy there is little hope that any new facts will influence them. The dead tell no tales. The living fear to speak, lest they fall victims to the humane theories of Beder Khan and Nejib Pasha.

"Will England now insist upon the protection of the Christian? She is morally bound to. Four times has she saved the Ottoman Empire from destruction, and the civilized world looks to her for a fulfilment of her high mission in the East.

"May British public opinion compel British public men to action!"

To make this chapter a little more complete for reference, I add a passing allusion to three other outrages not included in the above list, which takes account of no massacres of less than ten thousand victims at once.

OUTRAGES IN CRETE IN 1866-7.

On July 21, 1867, the British, Russian, French, and Italian Consuls at Canea, Crete, sent the following identical telegram to their several governments: "Massacres of women and children have broken out in the interior of the island. The authorities can neither put down the insurrection nor stay the course of these atrocities. Humanity would imperatively demand the immediate suspension of hostilities, or the transportation to Greece of the women and children."

The number of relieving ships sent to Crete in obedience to this accord was four French, three Russian, two Italian, three Austrian, and one Prussian.[1]

OUTRAGES IN ARMENIA IN 1877.

The writer is C. B. Norman, special correspondent of *The London Times*, who says in his preface:

"In my correspondence to the *Times* I made it a rule to report nothing but what came under my own personal observation, or facts confirmed by European evidence.

---

[1] U. S. Consul Stillman's *The Cretan Insurrection of* 1866-7-8. Henry Holt & Co., 1874.

"A complete list it is impossible for me to obtain, but from all sides—from Turk and Armenian alike—

A HIGHWAY IN ARMENIA.

I hear piteous tales of the desolation that reigns throughout Kurdistan — villages deserted, towns abandoned, trade at a standstill, harvest ready for the sickle, but none to gather it in, husbands mourning their dishonored wives, parents their murdered children; and this is not the work of a power whose policy of selfish aggression no man can defend, but the ghastly acts of Turkey's irregular soldiery on Turkey's most peaceable inhabitants,—acts the perpetrators of which are well known, and yet are allowed to go unpunished. . . .

"A bare recital of the horrors committed by these demons is sufficient to call for their condign punishment. The subject is too painful to need any coloring, were my feeble pen enabled to give it."

A few, out of many cases reported by Mr. Norman are given:

"This gang also attacked the village of Kordjotz, violating the women, and sending off all the virgins to their hills; entering the church they burned the Bible and sacred pictures; placing the communion-cup on the altar, they in turn defiled it, and divided the church plate amongst themselves. . . .

"Sheik Obaidulah's men rivalled their comrades under the flag of Jelaludeen; these latter operated between Van and Faik Pasha's camp. They attacked and robbed the villages of Shakbabgi and Adnagantz, carrying off all boys and virgins. At Kushartz they did the same, and killing 500 sheep, left them to rot in the streets, and then fired the place. Khosp, Jarashin, and Asdvadsadsan, Boghatz, and Aregh suffered in like manner; the churches were despoiled and desecrated, graves dug up, young of both sexes carried off, what grain they could not transport was destroyed, and the inhabitants driven naked into the fields, to gaze with horror on their burning homesteads."[1]

THE MASSACRE OF THE YEZIDIS NEAR MOSUL, 1892.

"The Yezidis are a remnant of a heathen sect, who have never been converted to the Moslem faith.

"Their holy place is not far from the city of Mo-

---

[1] C. B. Norman, *Armenia and the Campaign of 1877*, pp. 293-298. London: Cassell, Petter, & Galpin, 1879.

sul, one day's journey, and their principal villages are also close by. In the summer of 1892 the Sultan sent a special officer, called Ferik Pasha, to Mosul to correct certain abuses in the government, to collect all back taxes, and to convert the Yezidis. His authority was absolute, the Vali Pasha of the city being subject to his orders.

"In reference to his work among the Yezidis, he, it was generally reported, was to get a certain sum per capita for every convert made.

"He first sent priests among them to convert them to the "true faith." They not succeeding, he very soon gave them the old alternative of the Koran or the sword. Still not submitting, he sent his soldiers, under command of his son, who put to the sword all who, not able to escape, refused to accept Mohammed. Their villages were burned, many were killed in cold blood, some were tortured, women and young girls were outraged or carried off to harems, and other atrocities, too horrible to relate, were perpetrated.

"Those who escaped made their way to the mountains of Sinjar, where, together with their brethren of the mountains, they intrenched themselves and successfully defended themselves until the spring of 1893 against the government troops which had been sent against them.

"This massacre was reported to the French Government by M. Siouffi, Consul at that time in Mosul, and to the English Government by Mr. Parry, who was in that region under the instructions of the Archbishop of Canterbury.

"The Yezidis who remained in their villages on the plain had Moslem priests set over them to instruct them in the Moslem faith. They were compelled to attend prayers and nominally become Mohammedans; but in secret they practised their own rites and declared that they were still Yezidis."[1]

After the massacre of the Yezidi peasants in 1892 an English lady of rank, visiting Mosul, was refused permission by the Pasha to travel through the Yezidi district, lest she witness the dreadful results of the massacre.[2]

The writer in *The Independent* of January 31st, gives this explanation:

"The *reason* of the recurrence of massacres in Turkey is the fanatical intolerance of the Moslem populace and their hatred to Christianity, unrestrained and often fomented by Turkish officials.

"Lord Stratford de Redcliffe, the ablest and best friend Turkey ever had, who believed that 'England should befriend Turkey in order to reform her,' says:[3]

"'Turkey is weak, fanatical, and misgoverned. The Eastern question is a fact, a reality of indefinite duration. Like a volcano it has intervals of rest; but its outbreaks are frequent, their occasions uncertain, and their effects destructive' (p. 6).

"'Did not the massacres in Syria in 1860 come upon us by surprise? . . . Have we any substantial security against the recurrence of similar horrors, of a similar necessity, and of a similar hazard?' (p. 79).

---

[1] *The Independent*, January 17, 1895.
[2] *Ibid.*, January 31, 1895.   [3] *The Eastern Question.*

"'The position of the Ottoman Empire is one of natural determination toward a state of exhaustive weakness' (p. 97).

"'Ill fares the country where neither strong hand nor willing heart is to be found' (p. 104).

"A joint Commission is now *en route* to investigate the Sassoun massacres. Will any good come from it? Doubtful. Lord Stratford says (p. 117):

"'We know not how soon or where the kites may be again collected by a massacre or insurrection. . . . Such occasional meetings [of Commissions] have their portion of inconvenience and risk. Their failure is discreditable; the effect of their success, at best, transient and partial. The *evils* they are meant to correct are themselves the offspring of one pervading evil, the source of which is in Constantinople.'"

CHAPTER VIII.

ISLAM AS A FACTOR OF THE PROBLEM.

IT is with reluctance that I approach this side of the question. It is not desirable that the subject be complicated or embittered by religious animosities. But unfortunately these animosities do exist and have always formed a primary and essential feature in all the relations of the Turks with their Christian subjects. A writer who styles himself "Diplomatist," in a recent review article of considerable merit,[1] with a stroke of the pen, disposes of this phase of the subject by characterizing it as "pure moonshine." But real diplomatists do not find it so easy to dispose of, nor do the great historians treat it as moonshine. The fanatical gleam that I have often caught in the eye of Turks and Kurds was never suggestive to me of the mild rays of the lunar orb, but seemed rather like a gleam from the political Crescent, whose baleful influence dominates the East.

The question is not concerning the merits of Mohammed or of Mohammedanism in the abstract. I have a profound respect for the Prophet of Arabia, who might have been another Apostle Paul, but for the fact that the corrupt church of that day failed

[1] *New Review* for January, 1895.

to give that young and ardent seeker after God a true and worthy conception of Christianity. I would fain admit the high conception of the Mohammedan ideal, portrayed so skilfully by Mr. R. Bosworth Smith in his lectures before the Royal Institution of Great Britain.

But such considerations are irrelevant to the present discussion, which is simply, What are the practical bearings of Islam upon the question of reform or of reconstruction in Turkey?

As has been already shown in Chapter VI., the Ottoman Government is a *politico-religious system*. This is the necessary constitution of any Mohammedan sovereign state, but the conception has special force and vitality in Turkey, whose Sovereign claims to be the successor of Mohammed, and thus the Calif of the Mohammedan world. The whole fabric of the Turkish Empire rests on a religious foundation. This religious foundation is not the general religious principle in man, but the particular form of religion established by Mohammed.

To what *extent*, now, does Islam enter into the political structure? We find on investigation that it is part and parcel of the bone and sinew of the organism in Turkey called the State,—called so by courtesy on account of its faint analogy to what is understood in other countries by that name. The Turkish army is exclusively a Mohammedan army, the national festivals are Mohammedan festivals, the official calendar is a Mohammedan calendar, both as to year and month, the laws are based on the Koran and Mohammedan tradition, the expounders of the law are Mohammedan judges, and even testimony is a religious act of which only true believers are, in the nature of the case, capable. It is not denied that the testimony of Christians is allowed to be *given* in Turkish courts, but that does not signify that it is *valid* evidence in the eyes of the Court, especially when a Mohammedan is involved. Even the different formulæ used show this. In the case of a Mohammedan it is, "His Lordship, So and So, testified to the face of God"; in the case of a Christian it is, "Mr. Blank stated."

In Article 63 of the Treaty of Berlin we read Turkey's solemn (it is hard to suppress a smile) promise to the European Powers in regard to the rights of Christians before the law: *"All shall be allowed to give evidence before the courts without distinctions of creed."* The practical application of the above clause is shown in the official reports of British Consuls.[1]

Mr. Wilson, Consul-General in Anatolia, writes:

"In the greater portion of Anatolia, though Christian evidence may be received, no weight is attached to it. When Moslem and Christian evidence are opposed to each other, the latter is disregarded. For instance, three Christians are travelling along a road, and one of them is robbed by a man well known to all of them; in the action which ensues, the robber has only to prove an *alibi* by two Moslem false witnesses to gain his case."

---

[1] These extracts are from *Blue-Book*, Turkey, No. 8 (1881), pp. 57-110, as quoted by the high authority, M. Rolin-Jaequemyns, in his *Armenia, the Armenians, and the Treaties*, pp. 74-76. London: John Heywood, 1891.

Mr. Chermside, Vice-Consul at Sivas, writes:

"As regards the acceptance of Christian testimony, theoretically is it accepted in all *Nizam* courts. Hearing testimony, however, and attaching the relative importance to it that, from its tenor and consistency, it is entitled to, are very different matters; and there is no doubt that, especially in civil cases, tradition, sympathy, and education prejudice the *Hakim*[1] against it—sentimental considerations, however, are not proof against the love of gain."

According to the latter part of this quotation, the spirit which animates the courts of Asia Minor may be defined as fanaticism tempered by corruption. The following is the opinion of Mr. Everett, Vice-Consul at Erzerum : " The first consideration of the administrators of justice is the amount of money that can be extorted from an individual, and the second is his creed." The only doubt as to the morality of the Turkish magistrates appears to be whether they are more corrupt than fanatical, or more fanatical than corrupt.

The injustice done to Christians even in commercial transactions is shown by Mr. Bilotti, Consul at Trebizond:

"Christian evidence is accepted in the town of Trebizond, but I am assured in the districts, that though the same principle is admitted, no Mussulman has ever been condemned on the testimony of Christians; so much so, that the latter are in the

---

[1] The *Hakim*, who is a member of the religious body of *Ulemas*, presides over the lower court (Bidayet), which is to be found in every *caza* (hundred), and also over the *Sandjak* or district court.

habit of having their bonds witnessed only by Mussulmans."

Much is said in regard to the truthfulness of the Turks. Consul-General Wilson writes: "From the peculiar value of Moslem evidence, most of the false witnesses are Turks."

As a matter of fact, we thus see that the millions of Christians in Turkey neither are nor can be considered and treated as citizens of the state, simply because they do not belong to the religion of the foreign invaders who rule them. No degree of loyalty can secure for non-Moslems admission to the army. Christians are rapidly being excluded from even the humblest positions in the civil lists also, except from such as Mohammedans are incompetent to fill. The status of the Christian before the law is that of an alien in regard to his own rights, and of a slave as far as the interests of Mohammedans are concerned.

And yet we are told that the Ottoman Turks are tolerant of the members of other faiths. This is true in the same sense that the stomach is spoken of as being "tolerant" of certain easily digestible articles of food. Yes, so long as Christians submit to all forms of oppression, and make no claims in regard to rights which are generally supposed to belong to all men, they are gladly tolerated.

That the discrimination against Christian subjects is due to their religious belief, is, further, clearly shown by the fact that Mohammedans, who abandon the creed of the government, immediately forfeit their special privileges, and even incur punishment as criminals. Apostacy from Islam is treason to the Sultan. Converts to Christianity are arrested and imprisoned. In the rare instances when foreign governments venture to inquire into such cases, the Ottoman authorities blandly insist that they care nothing for the man's religion, but that he must be arrested for "avoiding conscription," or on some other fictitious charge. He is, thereupon, hurried off to some distant military post, or finds a living grave in an unknown dungeon.

Such is the politico-religious organization called the Ottoman Government. Can this union of Church and State be dissolved? It can not be. The bond which unites them, according to Mohammedan doctors, is vital, as in the case of the Siamese twins.

Inasmuch as the bond cannot be cut, the only remaining hope must be in improving the health of the two bodies thus indissolubly united. Unfortunately, no change can be hoped for in the case of either part of this dual patient. *Mohammedanism at its birth was a malformation*, to say the least, and will continue so even though restored to a state of perfect health. In the opinion of every orthodox Mohammedan, the Koran is a "perfect revelation of the will of God, sufficient and final," and "Islam is a separate, distinct, and absolutely exclusive religion."

As attempts are frequently made to convey a contrary impression on this point, I quote the words of President George Washburn, of Robert College, Constantinople, an impartial student of Islam, who for thirty-five years has observed its practical workings in the Ottoman Empire. At the World's Parliament of Religions, in Chicago, 1893, he read a paper on "The Points of Contact and Contrast between Christianity and Mohammedanism." His whole treatment is remarkable for its judicial fairness, and his paper is commended to the reader who may desire a brief, comprehensive, and fair estimate of Islam.

To the question whether Mohammedanism has been in any way modified, since the time of the Prophet, by its contact with Christianity, Dr. Washburn thinks that every orthodox Moslem would answer in the negative. He adds: "It is very important to bear in mind that there are nominal Mohammedans who are theists, and others who are pantheists of the Spinoza type. There are also some small sects who are rationalists, but after the fashion of old English Deism rather than of the modern rationalism. The Deistic rationalism is represented in that most interesting work of Justice Ameer Ali, *The Spirit of Islam*. He speaks of Mohammed as Xenophon did of Socrates, and he reveres Christ also, but he denies that there was anything supernatural in the inspiration or lives of either, and claims that Hanife and the other Imams corrupted Islam, as he thinks Paul the apostle did Christianity; but this book does not represent Mohammedanism, any more than Renan's *Life of Jesus* represents Christianity. These small rationalistic sects are looked upon by all orthodox Moslems as heretics of the worst description."

Although the Scriptures of the Old and New

Testaments happen to be mentioned one hundred and thirty-one times in the Koran, they are only quoted twice. The fundamental doctrines of Christianity, such as the Incarnation, the Trinity, the Atonement, and the Resurrection of Christ are specifically repudiated in the Koran.

The reform of Islam as a system is, therefore, not within the range of possibility. How about the reform of the Ottoman Government? On this point I yield the floor to the great historian E. A. Freeman, who will close the debate [1]:

"There are some people who say the Turks are no doubt very bad, but that the Christians are just as bad, and have done things just as cruel. Now, as a matter of fact, this is not true; and, if it were true, it would be another reason for setting the Christians free; for if they are as bad as the Turk, it is the Turk who has caused their badness. While other nations have been improving, the Turk has kept them from improving. Take away the Turk who hinders improvement, and they will improve like the others. The slave never has the virtues of a freeman; it is only by setting him free that he can get them.

"When we point out the evils of the rule of the Turk, some people tell us that Christian rulers in past times have done things quite as bad as the Turks. This is partly true, but not wholly. No Christian government has ever gone on for so long a time ruling as badly as the Turk has ruled. But it is true that Christian governments have in past times

[1] *The Turks in Europe.*

done particular acts, which were as bad as the acts of the Turks. But this argument, too, cuts the other way; for Christian governments have left off doing such acts, while the Turks go on doing them still. The worst Christian government is better now than it was one hundred years ago, or five hundred years ago. The rule of the Turk is worse now than it was one hundred years ago, or five hundred years ago. That is to say, the worst Christian government can reform, while the Turk cannot.

"It is sometimes said that we ought not to set free the Christians for fear that they should do some harm to the Mohammedans who would be left in their land. Now, if the question were really put, Shall a minority of oppressors go on oppressing the people of the land, or shall the majority of the people of the land turn round and oppress the minority who have hitherto oppressed them?—this last would surely be the lesser evil of the two. But there is no ground for any such fear. No one wishes to hurt any Mohammedan who will live peaceably and not hurt Christians. No one wishes that any man, merely because he is a Mohammedan, should be in any way worse off than a Christian, or be put under any disability as compared with a Christian. There is no reason why he should be. For the Mohammedan religion, though it does not command that Christians shall be persecuted, does command that Christians shall be treated as subjects of Mohammedans. But the Christian religion in no way commands that Mohammedan shall be treated as the subject of Christian. Christians and Mohammedans cannot live together on equal terms under a Mohammedan government, because the Mohammedan religion forbids that they should; but Mohammedans and Christians may perfectly well live together under a Christian government. They do so under the governments both of England and of Russia. The few Mohammedans who are left in Greece and in Servia are in no way molested; there are mosques both at Chalkis and at Belgrade. But it is foolish to argue, as some people do, that because men of different religions can live together under a Christian government, therefore they can live together under a Mohammedan government; for both reason and the nature of the Mohammedan religion prove that it is not so. . . .

"The Turk came in as an alien and barbarian encamped on the soil of Europe. At the end of five hundred years, he remains an alien and barbarian encamped on soil which he has no more made his own than it was when he first took Kallipolis. His rule during all that time has been the rule of strangers over enslaved nations in their own land. It has been the rule of cruelty, faithlessness, and brutal lust; it has not been government, but organized brigandage. His rule cannot be reformed. While all other nations get better and better, the Turk gets worse and worse. And when the chief powers of Europe join in demanding that he should make even the smallest reform, he impudently refuses to make any. If there was anything to be said for him before the late Conference, there is nothing to be said for him now. For an evil

which cannot be reformed, there is one remedy only
—to get rid of it. Justice, reason, humanity, demand that the rule of the Turk in Europe should be got rid of; and the time for getting rid of it has now come."

ARMENIAN REBELS WHO WOULD NOT PAY TAXES.

This was written seventeen years ago with reference to the discontinuance of the Ottoman power in Europe. Does it not now apply with equal force to the discontinuance of the same régime in Armenia?

CHAPTER IX.

GLADSTONE ON THE ARMENIAN MASSACRE AND ON TURKISH MISRULE.

ON the eighty-fifth anniversary of Mr. W. E. Gladstone's birth, December 29, 1894, a deputation of members of the National Church of Armenia presented to his son, the Rev. Stephen Gladstone, rector of Hawarden, a silver gilt chalice for the use of the church, in memory of the ex-Premier's sympathy with and assistance to the Armenian people. On that occasion Mr. Gladstone made a long and eloquent speech, in the course of which — after thanking the deputation for their token of sympathy and their grateful references to himself — he said :

"Well, Mr. Stevenson — I address myself now perhaps more particularly to you and to my own countrymen, to any of them who will take notice of the deputation. I have said that in my opinion this manifestation from the Armenian community in England and in Paris was, on my part at least, quite undeserved. I have done nothing for you in circumstances of great difficulty, and that, let me assure you, has not been owing to indifference. I will explain the cause in very few words. Rumors went abroad, growing more and more authenticated, which represented a state of horrible and indescribable outrage in Armenia. The impulse of every man in circumstances of that kind is to give way to a burst of strong feeling, but I had the conviction that in a grave case of this kind every nation is best and most properly represented by its government, which is the organ of the nation, and which has the right to speak with the authority of the nation.

"And do not let me be told that one nation has no authority over another. Every nation, and if need be every human being, has authority on behalf of humanity and of justice. (Hear, hear.) These are principles common to mankind, and the violation of which may justly, at the proper time, open the mouths of the very humblest among us. But in such cases as these we must endeavor to do injustice to no one, and the more dreadful the allegations may be, the more strictly it is our duty not to be premature in assuming their truth, but to wait for an examination of the case, and to see that what we say, we say upon a basis of ascertained facts.

"Well, gentlemen, it was, my fate—my fortune, I think—about eighteen years ago to take an active part with regard to other outrages which first came up in the shape of rumor, but were afterwards too horribly verified, in Bulgaria; but I never stirred in regard to those outrages until in the first place, their existence and their character had been established by indisputable authority; and, secondly, until I had found myself driven to absolute despair in regard to any hopes that I could entertain of a proper representation of British feeling on the part of the government which was then in office. You will see, therefore, that my conduct on this occasion has not been inconsistent with what I then did (hear, hear), and it does not imply, old as I am, that my feelings have been deadened in regard to matters of such a dreadful description. (Cheers.)

"Now I remained silent because I had full confidence that the government of the Queen would do its duty, and I still entertain that confidence. Its power and influence are considerable; at the same time they are limited. It is not in the power of this country, acting singly, to undertake to represent humanity at large, and to inflict, even upon the grossest wrong-doers, the punishments that their crimes may have deserved; but there is such a thing as the conscience of mankind at large, and the conscience is not limited even to Christendom. (Hear, hear.) And there is a great power in the collected voice of outraged humanity. What happened in Bulgaria? The Sultan and his government absolutely denied that anything wrong had been done. Yes, but their denial was shattered by the force of facts. The truth was exhibited to the world. It was thought an extravagance at the time when I said: 'It is time that the Turk and all his belongings should go out of Bulgaria bag and baggage.' They did go out of Bulgaria, and they went out of a good deal besides. But, quite independent of any sentiment of right, justice, or humanity, common sense and common prudence ought to have taught them not to repeat the infernal acts which disgraced the year 1876, so far as Turkey was concerned. (Cheers.)

"Now, it is certainly true that we have not arrived at the close of this inquiry, and I will say nothing to assume that the allegations will be verified. At the same time I cannot pretend to say that there is no reason to anticipate an unfavorable issue. On the contrary, the intelligence which has reached me tends to a conclusion which I still hope may not be verified, but tends strongly to a conclusion to the general effect that the outrages and the scenes and abominations of 1876 in Bulgaria have been repeated in 1894 in Armenia. As I have said, I hope it is not so, and I will hope to the last, but if it is so it is time that one general shout of execration, not of men, but of deeds, one general shout of execration directed against deeds of wickedness, should rise from outraged humanity, and should force itself into the ears of the Sultan of Turkey and make him sensible, if anything can make him sensible, of the madness of such a course.

"The history of Turkey has been a sad and painful history. That race has not been without remarkable and even in some cases fine qualities, but from too many points of view it has been a scourge to the world, made use of, no doubt, by a wise Providence for the sins of the world. If these tales of murder, violation, and outrage be true, then it will follow that they cannot be overlooked, and they cannot be made light of. I have lived to see the Empire of Turkey in Europe reduced to less than one half of what it was when I was born, and why? Simply because of its misdeeds—a great record written by the hand of Almighty God, in whom the

Turk, as a Mohammedan, believes, and believes firmly —written by the hand of Almighty God against injustice, against lust, against the most abominable cruelty; and if—and I hope, and I feel sure, that the government of the Queen will do everything that can be done to pierce to the bottom of this mystery, and to make the facts known to the world—if, happily —I speak hoping against hope—if the reports we have read are to be disproved or to be mitigated, then let us thank God; but if, on the other hand, they be established, then I say it will more than ever stand before the world that there is no lesson, however severe, that can teach certain people the duty, the prudence, the necessity of observing in some degree the laws of decency, and of humanity, and of justice, and that if allegations such as these are established, it will stand as if it were written with letters of iron on the records of the world, that such a government as that which can countenance and cover the perpetration of such outrages is a disgrace in the first place to Mahomet, the Prophet whom it professes to follow, that it is a disgrace to civilization at large, and that it is a curse to mankind. (Cheers.) Now, that is strong language.

"Strong language ought to be used when facts are strong, and ought not to be used without strength of facts. I have counselled you still to retain and to keep your judgment in suspense, but as the evidence grows and the case darkens, my hopes dwindle and decline; and as long as I have a voice I hope that voice, upon occasions, will be uttered on behalf of humanity and truth." (Cheers.)[1]

[1] *The London Times*, Weekly Edition Jan. 14, 1895.

In a remarkable paper entitled *Bulgarian Horrors and the Question of the East* called forth by the atrocities in 1876, Mr. Gladstone sums up some of the qualities of the Turkish race and of Turkish rule as follows:[1]

"Let me endeavor very briefly to sketch, in the rudest outline, what the Turkish race was and what it is. It is not a question of Mohammedanism simply, but of Mohammedanism compounded with the peculiar character of a race. They are not the mild Mohammedans of India, nor the chivalrous Saladins of Syria, nor the cultured Moors of Spain. They were, upon the whole, from the black day when they first entered Europe, the one great anti-human specimen of humanity. Wherever they went, a broad line of blood marked the track behind them; and, as far as their dominion reached, civilization disappeared from view. They represented everywhere government by force as opposed to government by law. For the guide of this life they had a relentless fatalism; for its reward hereafter, a sensual paradise.

"They were, indeed, a tremendous incarnation of military power. This advancing curse menaced the whole of Europe. It was only stayed—and that not in one generation, but in many—by the heroism of the European population of those very countries part of which form at this moment the scene of war, and the anxious subject of diplomatic action. In the olden time all Western Christendom sympathized with the resistance to the common enemy; and even during the hot and fierce struggles of the Reforma-

[1] Reprinted from *The Christian Register*, Boston, Dec. 1, 1894.

KURDISH HAMIDIÉH SOLDIERS EXECUTING THE "SWORD DANCE."

tion there were prayers, if I mistake not, offered up in the English churches for the success of the emperor—the head of the Roman Catholic power and influence—in his struggles with the Turk.

"But, although the Turk represented force as opposed to law, yet not even a government of force can be maintained without the aid of an intellectual element such as he did not possess. Hence there grew up what has been rare in the history of the world, a kind of tolerance in the midst of cruelty, tyranny, and rapine. Much of Christian life was contemptuously let alone, much of the subordinate functions of government was allowed to devolve upon the bishops; and a race of Greeks was attracted to Constantinople which has all along made up, in some degree, the deficiencies of Turkish Islam in the element of mind, and which at this moment provides the Porte with its long-known and, I must add, highly esteemed ambassador in London. Then there have been, from time to time, but rarely, statesmen whom we have been too ready to mistake for specimens of what Turkey might become, whereas they were, in truth, more like *lusus naturæ*, on the favorable side,—monsters, so to speak, of virtue or intelligence. And there were (and are) also, scattered through the community, men who were not, indeed, real citizens, but yet who have exhibited the true civic virtues, and who would have been citizens, had there been a true polity around them. Besides all this, the conduct of the race has gradually been brought more under the eye of Europe, which it has lost its power to resist or to defy; and its central government, in conforming perforce to many of the forms and traditions of civilization, has occasionally caught something of their spirit. . . .

"I entreat my countrymen, upon whom far more than perhaps any other people of Europe it depends, to require and to insist that our government, which has been working in one direction, shall work in the other, and shall apply all its vigor to concur with the other states of Europe in obtaining the extinction of the Turkish executive power in Bulgaria. Let the Turks now carry away their abuses in the only possible manner—namely, by carrying off themselves. Their Zaptichs and their Mudirs, their Bimbashis and their Yuzbachis, their Kaimakams and their Pashas,—one and all, bag and baggage,—shall, I hope, clear out from the province they have desolated and profaned. This thorough riddance, this most blessed deliverance, is the only reparation we can make to the memory of those heaps on heaps of dead; to the violated purity alike of matron, of maiden, and of child; to the civilization which has been affronted and shamed; to the laws of God, or, if you like, of Allah; to the moral sense of mankind at large. There is not a criminal in a European jail, there is not a cannibal in the South Sea Islands, whose indignation would not arise and overboil at the recital of that which has been done; which has too late been examined, but which remains unavenged; which has left behind all the foul and all the fierce passions that produced it; and which may again spring up, in another murderous harvest, from the soil soaked and reeking with blood, and in the air tainted with every imaginable deed of crime and shame. *That such things should be done once is a damning disgrace to the portion of our race which did them, that a door should be left open for their ever-so-barely possible repetition would spread that shame over the whole.*¹ Better, we may justly tell the Sultan, almost any inconvenience, difficulty, or loss associated with Bulgaria,

> 'Than thou reseated in thy place of light,
> The mockery of thy people and their bane.'

"We may ransack the annals of the world; but I know not what research can furnish us with so portentous an example of the fiendish misuse of the powers established by God 'for the punishment of evil-doers, and for the encouragement of them that do well.' No government ever has so sinned; none has so proved itself incorrigible in sin, or, which is the same, so impotent for reformation. If it be allowable that the executive power of Turkey should renew, at this great crisis, by permission or authority of Europe, the charter of its existence in Bulgaria, then there is not on record, since the beginnings of political society, a protest that man has lodged against intolerable misgovernment, or a stroke he has dealt at loathsome tyranny, that ought not henceforth forward to be branded as a crime."

¹ And yet England by the Cyprus Convention pledged all her resources to *keep the door open*, and the repetition thus made possible has occurred. Author.

CHAPTER X.

WHO ARE THE ARMENIANS?

THAT a field so rich in possibilities for the student of history, ethnology, or language as Armenia and Kurdistan should have remained as yet so little explored, is due, no doubt, to three causes[1]: first, the apparent loss of significance of the Armenian nation, which now, like Poland, seems but a stranded wreck in the stream of history; second, to her geographical isolation and the danger and hardship of travel in that region[2]; third, to the linguistic obstacles to be overcome.

So little clear and accurate information about the Armenians is readily accessible that the following brief outline is offered in the hope of meeting this want at the present time.

HISTORY—The Armenian race belongs to the

[1] "Kurdistan abounds in antiquities of the most varied and interesting character. . . . It may indeed be asserted that there is no region of the East at the present day which deserves a more careful scrutiny and promises a richer harvest to the antiquarian explorer than the lands inhabited by the Kurds from Erzeroum to Kirmanshahan."—Major-General H. C. Rawlinson, *Encyc. Britannica*, article on "Kurdistan."

[2] Mrs. Isabella Bird Bishop, *Journeys in Persia and Kurdistan*. 2 vols. New York: Putnam's, 1891. London: John Murray.

Japhetic branch of the human family, falling under the same category as the inhabitants of India and Persia, who form the Aryans of Asia. The Armenian language proves this by its affinity with the Indo-Germanic tongues. Their physiognomy and physical constitution connect them with the best types of Caucasian stock. Their manners and customs, as well as their religious beliefs, in heathenism, were similar to those of the Assyrians and Chaldeans, of the Medes and Persians, and, still later, of the Parthians.

These people call themselves Haik, after Haig, the most celebrated of their ancient kings, and their land Haiasdan. Their national legends, fortified in their eyes by the Bible, make Haig descend from Ashkenaz or Togarmah, children of Gomer, a patriarch of the line of Japhet.[1] Foreigners applied to them the name Armenians, derived from King Aram, said to be a descendant of Haig, who made great conquests.[2]

The earliest biblical mention of this land is the statement that the ark " rested upon the mountains of Ararat," a term which evidently refers to a district rather than a peak.[3] Another scriptural allusion is in connection with Sennacherib, whose parricidal sons are said to have escaped, 681 B. C., "into the land of Armenia."[4] Ezekiel also refers to Armenia under the name Togarmah, as furnishing Tyre with

---

[1] Gen. x., 2, 3.
[2] Moses of Khorene, *History*, Bk. i., chap. 12.
[3] Gen. viii., 4.
[4] Heb. Ararat, 2 Kings xix., 37 ; Isa. xxxvii., 38.

horses and mules, a product for which it is still noted.¹ Tigranes I. is said to have been an ally of Cyrus the Great in overthrowing the Babylonians, and thus in liberating the Jews after their seventy years' captivity, 538 B. C. A foreshadowing of this event is probably found in the prophet Jeremiah: "Call together against her the kingdoms of Ararat, Minni, and Ashkenaz, . . . to make the land of Babylon a desolation without an inhabitant."²

In the famous inscriptions of the Achemenidæ, at Persepolis and at Behistun, the name Armenia is found in various forms, and the Armenian tributaries march after the Cappadocians to render homage to the great king.³

Herodotus mentions the absorption of the Armenian Empire in that of Darius, 514 B. C., and a tribute of four hundred talents exacted.⁴

Xenophon's account of the retreat of the ten thousand through this mountainous region, in midwinter, and constantly harassed by enemies, is valuable, not only as a tribute to the splendid discipline and spirit of the Greeks, but for the light which it throws upon the ancient Armenians and Kurds, whose houses, domestic habits, and employments are the same in many respects even at the present day.⁵

Armenia was included in the conquests of Alexander, and afterwards submitted to the Seleucidæ of

---

¹ Ezek. xxvii., 14; also xxxviii., 6.
² Jer. li., 27-29; also l., 9, 41, 42.
³ Christian Lassen, *Die altpersischen Keil-Inschriften von Persepolis*, Bonn, 1836, pp. 86, 87.
⁴ *History*, Bk. iii., chap. 93.   ⁵ *Anabasis*, Bk. iv.

Syria. In 190 B. C., when Antiochus the Great was defeated by Scipio, Armenia revolted under Artaxias, who gave refuge to the exiled Hannibal. About 150 B. C., the great Parthian king, Mithridates I., established his brother Valarsaces in Armenia. The most celebrated king of this branch of the Arsacid family was Tigranes II., who, while aiding Mithridates of Pontus, was defeated by Pompey. After this, Tacitus says that the Armenians were almost always at war; with the Romans through hatred, and with the Parthians through jealousy.[1] Princes of this line continued to rule, however, until the Arsacidæ were driven from the Persian throne by the Sassanid Ardashir. Though frequently conquered by the kings of that dynasty, Armenia was enabled as often to re-assert her freedom by the help of Roman arms.

When Tiridates embraced Christianity, 276 A. D., the struggle became embittered by the introduction of a religious element, for the Persians were bigoted Zoroastrians. This condition reached a climax when the country was divided between the Romans and Persians, under Theodosius the Great, 390 A. D.

After the fall of the Sassanidæ, in the seventh century, Armenia was divided between the Greek Empire and the Saracens; but from 859 to 1045 it was again ruled by a native dynasty of vigorous princes, the Pagratidæ. This was brought to a close by the suspicious and short-sighted policy of the Byzantine emperors, one of whom, Constantine IX., at last overthrew the Armenian kingdom, thereby laying

---

[1] *Annales*, Bk. ii., ch. 56.

AN ARMENIAN TOMBSTONE OF A.D. 934.
Evidence of a high state of art.

open the whole eastern frontier to the invasion of the Seljouk Turks, who shortly before had begun their attacks, and who might have been successfully resisted by these hardy mountaineers. The result was fatal, both to Armenia, which was overrun, and to the Greek Empire; for by the battle of Manzikert, 1071 A. D., when Romanus IV. was defeated and made prisoner by Alp Arslan, the whole of Asia Minor was left at the mercy of the Seljouks.[1]

Rupen, a relative of the last Pagratid sovereign, escaped into Cilicia, and established the Rupenian dynasty, which was not extinguished until the death of Leon VI., 1393, an exile in Paris, and the last of the Armenian kings. The Rupenians had entered into alliance with the Crusaders. They welcomed the Mongolian hordes under Genghis Khan, early in the thirteenth century, and suffered the vengeance of the Mamelukes, 1375.

A graphic account of the cruelties of Timour the Tartar, who devastated Armenia at the close of the fourteenth century, has been left us by Thomas of Medzop. The last great calamity which fell upon the mother country happened in 1605, when Shah Abbas forcibly transplanted twelve thousand families to Ispahan in Persia.

THE ARMENIAN CHURCH.—It is the oldest of all national churches. Their legends claim that our Lord corresponded with King Abgarus of Edessa or Ur, and that the apostles Thaddæus and Bartholomew preached the Gospel to them. But the historical founder of the Armenian church was St. Gregory

---

[1] Tozer, *The Church and the Eastern Empire*, pp. 22, 86.

"The Illuminator,"[1] an Arsacid prince, related to King Tiridates (Dertad), who was consecrated Bishop of Armenia, at Cæsarea, in 302 A. D. The Armenian church is Episcopal in polity, and closely resembles the Greek in outward forms.

Misled by imperfect reports of the Council of Chalcedon, 451, which they were not able to attend on account of Persian persecutions, the Armenian bishops annulled its decrees in 536, thus gaining the credit of being Eutychians, which led to their gradual separation from the orthodox church, much to the satisfaction of the Persian ruler Chosroes. This estrangement was doubtless political as much as doctrinal, on account of the attempts at ecclesiastical supremacy by the churches of Constantinople and Rome. As far as her ecclesiastical writers are concerned, and her beautiful liturgy, the Armenian church is in general orthodox. Her heresy, in common with that of the rest of Christendom, is one of life rather than of doctrine. A chism in the Armenian church was brought about in the sixteenth century by Jesuit missionaries, who succeeded in detaching the community of Catholic Armenians from the mother church, of which the Catholicos at Etchmiadzin is recognized as the supreme head.

All Armenians—except perhaps the Catholic, whose allegiance has been transferred of course to Rome—still cherish a passionate attachment for the venerable church of their ancestors, to which they owe their identity as a people after the terrible vicis-

---

[1] Krikor " Loosavoritch," from which title the Armenian Gregorian church calls itself Loosavortchagan.

situdes of so many centuries. It is true that Armenians who have come under European influence, especially French, have to some extent become sceptical and indifferent to religion. But even such men still profess at least an outward loyalty, as a matter of sentiment, and because they believe the formal preservation of the Armenian church to be the condition of national union in the future as it has been in the past. It is, indeed, almost a political necessity, as the Ottoman Empire is now constituted.

It is to be hoped that the time will come when the children of the Armenian church of every shade will no longer look upon her as a mother frail and failing, yet to be treated with respect while she lasts; nor as a mother ignorant and bigoted beyond hope of reform; still less, as one heretical and to be abandoned for Rome. Rather, let all her sons rally around her and help her to fulfil her true spiritual mission. She will then renew her youth and again take her honored place in the front ranks of "the Church of the living God, which is the pillar and ground of the truth."

Would that the spirit of the grand and broad-minded man who is now the Catholicos at Etchmiadzin, His Holiness, Mugerditch Khrimian, might pervade the whole body of which he is the honored and beloved head. Less than a year ago, the author had the privilege of a long private interview with this venerable ecclesiastic, whose hand he kissed in oriental fashion, with respect for the man and for himself. His last words to me, found upon the title-page, were "*Husahadelu chenk*," meaning, "We must not despair"—a good motto for us all.

That the grand old church of "The Illuminator" should somewhat lose its hold on the mind and conscience of the rising generation at this stage of super-

THE CATHOLICOS OF ETCHMIADZIN, IN THE CAUCASUS,
Religious head of the Armenian Church.

ficial enlightenment is not strange. Her real merits are concealed, unfortunately, under a growth of superstition and ignorance which even the clergy admit, but lack the courage and ability to remove. These abuses, however, are not due to any demoralization of the Armenian race itself, but to its isolation, and to the repeated and terrible devastations that have checked its growth and reduced it to a condition of extreme poverty and helplessness.

No greater service could be rendered to the Armenian people than aid and encouragement in establishing institutions for the education of the clergy, who under present circumstances are their natural leaders. The twentieth century will bring, we hope, better political privileges. But unless, in the meantime, the ancient church has maintained her hold on the conscience of the rising generation, she is in danger of sinking into the position of the church in France.

By nature the Armenians are deeply religious, as their whole literature and history show. It has been a religion of the heart, not of the head. Its evidence is not to be found in metaphysical discussions and hair-splitting theology as in the case of the Greeks, but in a brave and simple record written with the tears of saints and illuminated with the blood of martyrs.

The seeds of a thorough and far-reaching reformation have been carefully sown and are already bearing fruit. The prospect of reform is brightened by three facts: first, the Armenian church is essentially democratic, and is not in bondage to any "infallible" human authority; second, her errors of doctrine and practice are not fundamental, and, having never been sanctioned by councils, but simply by custom and tradition, can in due time be discarded; third, she has always acknowledged the supreme authority of

THE SUBORDINATE CATHOLICOS OF AGHTAMAR, A TOOL OF THE TURKS.
Wearing the Sultan's highest decorations for services rendered.

the Bible, which is no longer a sealed book, having been translated into the modern tongue by American missionaries, very widely scattered, and at last gladly received by all classes. The demand for progress and reform is by no means confined to the so-called "evangelical" element, but is making itself heard even in the pulpits of the old church and in the secular press.

The Armenians, very numerous in ancient times, now number only about 4,000,000, of whom 2,500,000 are under the Sultan, 1,200,000 in Russia, 150,000 in Persia, and the rest widely scattered in many lands, but everywhere distinguished for their peaceable and enterprising character. They are the leading bankers, merchants, and skilled artisans of Turkey, and extensively engage in the various trades, manufactures, and agriculture as well. They love their native home and are yet destined to play an important part in the moral and material regeneration of western Asia.

The following estimate is from an experienced and discriminating authority, who is also a member of the Church of England :

" I have confessed already to a prejudice against the Armenians, but it is not possible to deny that they are the most capable, energetic, enterprising, and pushing race in Western Asia, physically superior, and intellectually acute, and *above all they are a race which can be raised in all respects to our own level, neither religion, color, customs, nor inferiority in intellect or force constituting any barrier between us.* Their shrewdness and aptitude for business are remarkable, and whatever exists of commercial enterprise in Eastern Asia Minor is almost altogether in their hands. They have singular elasticity, as their survival as a church and nation shows, and I cannot but think it likely that they may have some share in determining the course of events in the East, both politically and religiously. As Orientals they understand Oriental character and modes of thought as we never can, and if a new Pentecostal *afflatus* were to fall upon the educated and intelligent young men who are being trained in the colleges which the American churches have scattered liberally through Asia Minor, the effect upon Turkey would be marvellous. I think most decidedly that reform in Turkey must come through Christianity, and in this view the reform and enlightenment of the religion which has such a task before it are of momentous importance."[1]

LANGUAGE AND LITERATURE.—The Armenian grammar is analogous to that of other languages of the same origin. It has not the distinction of gender, but is rich in its declensions and conjugations. The accent of Armenian words is on the last syllable, and many of the strong consonantal sounds strike the ear of a foreigner with harshness, and defy his tongue. The rich native vocabulary has been increased by additions from languages with which it has come in contact. It possesses also, as the German, great facility in building compound words.

The earliest specimen of this language, though in the cuneiform character, is probably to be found in the tri-lingual inscriptions on the great citadel rock of Van, which have not yet been satisfactorily made out. The pre-Christian literature of Armenia, consisting of national songs, has entirely perished, ex-

[1] Mrs. Bishop, *Journeys in Persia and Kurdistan*, vol. ii., p. 336.

cept a few quotations. All that has come down to us is subsequent to the fourth century, and refers exclusively to history or religion. Poetry and fiction never greatly flourished among this serious race, always in the midst of danger or suffering.

The ancient Armenian version of the Bible, made by Mesrob, the inventor of their alphabet, and his disciples, early in the fifth century, has been called the queen of versions for its beauty, and, though not based on the Hebrew, is of some critical value in determining the readings of the Septuagint, of which it does not follow any known recension. Hundreds of other translations from Syriac and Greek writers soon followed, some of which are extant only in Armenian.

The fifth century, their Golden Age, was adorned by such classic writers as Yeznig of Goghp, who wrote most eloquently, in four books, against the Persian fire-worshippers, the Greek philosophers, the Marcion heresy, and the Manichæans; Goriun, the biographer of Mesrob; David, the philosopher and translator of Aristotle; Yeghishe, who relates the heroic struggle of Vartan for the Christian faith against the Persian Zoroastrians; Lazarus of Parb; and Moses of Khorene, their national historian. There follows a period of four centuries of literary barrenness, due to political disorder and schism.

Under the Rupenian dynasty there was a second period of literary brilliancy. Then flourished Nerses Schnorhali "The Gracious," an orator grafted upon the poet; as well as Nerses of Lampron, whose hymns also enrich the beautiful Armenian liturgy. The

Who are the Armenians? 145

annals of Matthew of Edessa give interesting facts about the first Crusade. Samuel of Ani, John

THE ISLAND MONASTERY OF AGHTAMAR, IN LAKE VAN.
One of many similar Armenian Monasteries still existing, rich in parchment manuscripts exposed to decay and vandalism.

Vanagan, Vartan the Great, and Thomas of Medzop wrote succeeding chronicles.

A third revival of Armenian letters was begun by

Mechitar of Sebaste (Sivas), who established an order of Catholic monks at the monastery of St. Lazarus in Venice, 1717. These fathers have won the interest and admiration of European scholars by their publication of Armenian classics, together with many learned original contributions. Other centres of literary activity are to be found in Vienna, Paris, and the Institute of Moscow, as well as the schools of Constantinople and Tiflis.

A list of authorities on Armenian subjects is given in Appendix E.

CHAPTER XI.

AMERICANS IN TURKEY, THEIR WORK AND INFLUENCE.

THE American missionaries in the Turkish Empire are brought into the discussion of almost every question that arises in that land. Especially is this true at present, in connection with the Armenian problem. So many wild and contradictory statements are made in regard to them, and the Protestant communities which are the direct results of their labors, that the mind of the public is more or less confused on the subject. The missionaries, and the many thousands who have gladly followed their leadership in intellectual, moral, and religious reform, *are* an important, though not a noisy or conspicuous element. For this reason, as well as on account of popular ignorance and hostile misrepresentation, they cannot be overlooked in any fair and adequate survey of the situation. The writer has long been familiar with this phase of the subject, and has a large mass of evidence and statistics at his command. *But he is not connected with any of the various missionary societies involved, and is alone responsible for the statements made in this or any other part of the volume.*

It is very important to note that charges against the missionaries, of disloyalty to the Sultan, have never been sustained for a moment, and that investigation has shown them to be obedient to the laws, and opposed to revolutionary sentiments upon the part of any of the subjects of the Empire. The highest officials have repeatedly borne public testimony to the valuable services of the Americans in educational, literary, medical and philanthropic lines. Even H. I. M. Sultan Abd-ul-Hamid has graciously given expression to his confidence in Americans as being free from any political designs, such as all Europeans are supposed to entertain.

Many are not aware of the great work already accomplished by American missionaries during the past seventy years in the Ottoman Empire, nor of the vast influence they have exerted, both directly and indirectly. They have been in many departments the pioneers of civilization. They have stuck to their posts, obscure or prominent, in peace or in war, in famine, plague and persecution. Pashas and diplomats and generals have sought their aid without fear of being misled or betrayed. But the messengers of the Cross have never been swerved from what they consider a "higher calling"—to instruct the ignorant, young and old, to counsel and reclaim the erring, to attend the sick and imprisoned, and to comfort the broken-hearted. To support these general statements, the reader must pardon a few statistics compiled from the latest official tables, showing the *direct results* of American missionary effort in Turkey.

STATISTICS OF AMERICAN MISSIONS IN TURKEY.[1]

The following figures, with the exception of the Press statistics, represent the work of the American Board (Congregational) and of the Presbyterian Board taken together.

The Congregational proportion constitutes about three fourths and the Presbyterian one fourth in all these figures, the work of the latter society being confined to Syria and Mosul.

THE FORCE.

Laborers.

Foreign missionaries	223
Native pastors, preachers, teachers, etc.	1,094
Total force of laborers	1,317
American missionaries to Turkey since 1821	550

[1] By far the largest part of foreign missionary work in Turkey has always been in the hands of Americans, although, of course, they neither claim nor have any monopoly in this respect. As a matter of fact there are many other large and successful missionary, benevolent, and educational enterprises conducted in that land by other foreign societies as well as individuals. The various Roman Catholic orders are strongly established in many parts, and are generally of French connections and introduce that language in their work as the Americans do English. The following is a partial list of other societies at work in Turkey: The British and Foreign Bible Society, the Church Missionary Society, the Bible Lands Missions Aid Society, the British Syrian Mission Schools and Bible Work, the Church of Scotland Mission to the Jews, the Society of Friends (both English and American), the Irish Presbyterian Mission, the Reformed Presbyterian Mission, and the German Deaconesses. In addition to all these agencies, there are many private and local schools and institutions that are doing excellent work, but of which only this general mention can here be made.

The statistics of Robert College, Constantinople, are not included in these tables, as that institution, though a child of American Missions, is independent of them.

Plant.

Value of property held by Americans, exclusive of churches, schools, etc., erected in the names of native subjects, with foreign aid, for which statistics are not available	$2,500,000

Annual Expenditure.

Appropriations from America	$225,000
From native sources	60,000
Total expenditure annually	$285,000
Total American expenditure from the first, at least	$10,000,000

THE RESULTS.

Religious.

Churches organized	155
Other stated preaching places	281
Total number of preaching places	436
Communicants (received on confession of faith)	13,528
Members of Protestant civil communities (adherents)	60,000
Average Sunday congregations	40,000
Sunday-school membership	35,000

Educational.

Colleges well equipped, for both sexes	5		
Theological seminaries	6	students	4,085
High-schools for boys } Boarding-schools for girls }	80		
Common schools for both sexes	530	··	23,315
Total schools of all grades	621	Students	27,400

There are six American institutions in Turkey incorporated under the laws of the United States, and controlled by trustees in that land.

Medical.

There is a well equipped American Medical College and Hospital at Beirut, and American missionary physicians treat, yearly, many thousands of patients of all classes and races throughout the land, both in their dispensaries and in private practice, at a nominal sum and very often gratuitously.

Publishing.

Both weekly and monthly newspapers are published by the American missionaries at Constantinople, in the Armenian, Turkish, Greek, and Bulgarian languages, and an Arabic weekly is published at Beirut.

The catalogue of editions of the Scriptures and of religious, educational, and miscellaneous books and tracts in various languages, which may be obtained at the American Bible House, Constantinople, contains separate titles to the number of about 1000. The publications in the catalogue of the Presbyterian Press at Beirut, mostly in Arabic, number 507. The number of copies of the Scriptures (entire or in part) put in circulation by the Levant Agency of the American Bible Society alone, 1847 to 1893, is 1,378,715. The number of copies of the Scriptures (entire or in part) *in languages and type available for Mohammedans*, put in circulation by the same Agency in 1893, was Osmanli-Turkish (Arabic type), 5,392 ; Arabic language (Arabic type), 34,077 ; total, 39,469.

The number of copies of Scriptures (entire or in part) circulated in Turkey since 1820 amounts to about 3,000,000. The number of copies of other books and tracts for the same period is about 4,000,000. The total number of copies of the Scriptures and of miscellaneous literature circulated is therefore about 7,000,000.

Even these large figures by no means measure the extent and significance of Protestant influence in Turkey. The idea and spirit of Protestantism has a breadth which cannot be measured or portrayed by figures. As a matter of convenience and political

ARMENIAN FAMILY, BITLIS.

necessity, and also to destroy unity of feeling and action among the subject peoples, all non-Moslem races were classified by Mohammed II., after the capture of Constantinople in 1453, according to their religious belief. These lines of division have always been strictly observed by the government in all its dealings with non-Moslems. Even many of the taxes are collected through ecclesiastical organizations. This policy of the government, together with the bitter persecution of Protestants by the older churches, led to the formation of a Protestant civil community in 1850, contrary to the original desire and instruction of the missionaries, and in spite of the protests of many evangelicals who preferred to retain connection with their ancestral church, but who were thrust out with violence and anathema.

The Protestant communities which then sprang up all over the Empire, were not ruled, as are the other Oriental churches, by hierarchical bodies. The missionaries, who are mostly Congregational or Presbyterian, while ready to advise and guide, have never exercised ecclesiastical control over their converts. The Protestants, in accordance with their inherent spirit and beliefs, have naturally organized their religious and civil communities on a simple representative basis, which has gradually developed independence of thought and character, and desire for progress.

We come now to the *indirect results* of missionary effort, namely, the stimulus of evangelical example and success upon the Gregorian and other communities including even the Mohammedans. The homes, schools, and churches of the missionaries have been open to all comers; their varied literature has gone everywhere; their aid in sickness, distress, and famine has always ignored race or creed. Many thousands of Armenians, Greeks, Syrians, Jacobites and others — Moslems being prevented by their rulers except in rare instances—have received education in Protestant schools, without changing their church relations. But, nevertheless, a deep impression has been made on these pupils by contact no less than by teaching, and this, together with a natural and worthy loyalty to their own institutions, has stirred up all the other races to higher ideals and efforts.[1]

The existence of a marked desire for progress by all classes is now clear, and that this is largely due to foreign missionaries is admitted by all[2]—gratefully by the Armenians and Christians generally, but often with chagrin by the Turks, who find themselves

[1] "The creation of churches, strict in their discipline, and protesting against the mass of superstitions which smother all spiritual life in the National Armenian Church, is undoubtedly having a very salutary effect far beyond the limited membership, and is tending to force reform upon an ancient church which contains within herself the elements of resurrection."—Mrs. Bishop, *Journeys in Persia and Kurdistan*, vol. ii., p. 336.

[2] Unhappily there are some who can see nothing but bigotry and mistakes in what the missionaries have done. Such characters are to be found among all races, as the following extract shows:

"It might be thought that here, [Missilonghi] on the spot where he [Byron] breathed his last, malignity would have held her accursed tongue; but it was not so. He had committed the fault, unpardonable in the eyes of political opponents, of attaching himself to one of the great parties that then divided Greece; and though he had given her all that man could give, in his own dying words, 'his time, his means, his health, and, lastly, his life,' the Greeks spoke of him with all the rancour and bitterness of party spirit. Even death had not won oblivion for his political offences; and I heard those who saw him die in her cause affirm that Byron was no friend to Greece."—Stephens, *Greece, Turkey, Russia, and Poland*, New York: Harper and Brothers, 1839.

being rapidly left behind in the forward march which they have been too stupid or too proud to fall in with. It is, however, very gratifying to see that the Mohammedan leaders in both Church and State are at length becoming aware of the marked intellectual awakening and substantial progress that education has quietly brought about among the Christian races. Robert College on the Bosphorus stands at the head of the many well equipped American institutions in Turkey which have largely contributed to these results.

We gladly recognize the wisdom and energy of His Majesty the present Sultan, in trying to establish Moslem schools throughout his empire, some of which are already quite large, creditable, and popular with the Turks. It cannot be doubted that these schools will lead ultimately to an awakening and a desire for reform and progress among Moslems which will make them no less restive under present conditions than are the non-Moslems to-day, and thus hasten the necessary reforms. While most hearty praise is due His Majesty for fostering and even forcing education among his Moslem subjects, it is greatly to be regretted that there is another side to this policy as carried out by his agents, namely, an equal zeal in curtailing and even closing, as far as possible, Christian schools.

The hostility of the Sublime Porte has been growing, just in proportion as the excellent results of American institutions, already enumerated, have appeared. Does the Turkish Government desire that its hostility be considered the most convincing proof of the success of disinterested efforts to benefit its subjects of all classes? And does it propose to continue to cripple and suppress such efforts? If so, it is not the two hundred and fifty American missionaries in her borders who will suffer, but the many schools and churches which they have planted and the many thousands of peaceable and hitherto loyal subjects, who have been taught in them to serve God as well as honor the king.

APPENDIX A.

A BIT OF AMERICAN DIPLOMACY IN TURKEY.

THE CASE.

(Foreign Relations of the United States, 1884, pp. 538-539.[1])

(Inclosure in No. 317.)

Mr. Wallace to Aarifi Pasha.

Note Verbale.

LEGATION OF THE UNITED STATES,
Constantinople, January 24, 1884.

The legation of the United States of America has the honor to invite the attention of his highness, the minister of foreign affairs, to the matters following :

By note No. 167, June 13, 1883, the legation informed his highness that two American citizens, traveling in the vilayet of Bitlis, had been set upon by Kurds, robbed, and left to die, and that the governor-general of the vilayet had manifested the most singular indifference about the affair, and might be fairly charged with responsibility for the escape of the malefactors. The suggestion was then made that his highness would serve the cause of humanity and justice by ordering the most energetic measures to be taken for the apprehension of the robbers.

By a communication, No. 71235, June 13, 1883, his highness was good enough to answer the note of the legation, and give the pleas-

---

[1] This is an exact copy of the official documents as published by the State Department, capitalization included.

ing intelligence that the governor-general had succeeded in discovering the goods taken from the two gentlemen, and that the robbers had been arrested and delivered up to justice. This information his highness reported as derived from the governor-general.

This report the legation found it necessary to correct; and for that purpose it addressed a second note to his highness, the minister of foreign affairs, No. 179, dated September 10, 1883, declaring that the robbers had not been arrested, and that the goods and money taken from Messrs. Knapp and Reynolds had been returned to them, but in small parts. Under impression that it was yet possible to obtain the powerful assistance of the Sublime Porte in bringing the thieves and assassins to justice, the legation in the same note proceeded to give the full particulars of the affair, both those connected with the assault and those descriptive of the action of the governor-general. Of the assault, it remarked that Messrs. Knapp and Reynolds, accepting the assurance of the governor-general that the roads were perfectly safe, set out on their journey without a guard of zaptiehs. They put up for a night at a house where there was present Moussa Bey, son of Meza Bey, an influential Kurdish chief. When they took their coffee they failed to send a cup of it to the said Moussa, who feeling himself insulted by the inattention, took four assistants and next day waylaid the gentlemen, one of whom, Mr. Knapp, they beat with clubs until they supposed him dead. Moussa Bey, with his own hand, cut down Dr. Reynolds, giving him ten cuts with a sword. The two were then bound and dragged into the bushes and there left to die. That there might be no excuse, such as that the murderers were unknown, the legation gave his highness the names of the subordinate assassins and their places of abode, Sherif Oglon Osman and Iskan Oglon Hassan, both of the village of Movnok. A third one was pointed out as the servant of Moussa Bey, living in the village of Kabian. Of the action of the governor-general the legation said further that when the affair was reported to him he made a show of action by sending zaptiehs to arrest the robbers, but, singular to remark, he selected Meza Bey, the father of Moussa, to take charge of the party. Going to the village of Auzont, Meza Bey pointed out four Kurds of another tribe as the guilty men, took them into custody and carried them for identification to Messrs. Knapp and Reynolds, who said they were not the assailants.

During the night, in Aozon, a bundle was thrown through a window into a room occupied by the police, which on examination proved to contain a portion of the stolen goods. With this the governor-general rested from his efforts and dispatched to his highness the minister of foreign affairs, that the stolen goods were recovered and returned, and the felons captured and punished. This report, the legation took the liberty of informing his highness, was not true, also that the chief of the assassins, Moussa Bey, was still at large; and to emphasize its statement, the legation further said to his highness, that the details it communicated were current through all the region of Bitlis, having been first given out by Moussa himself. The legation then, in the same note, exposed the maladministration of the governor-general in language plain as respect for his highness, the minister, and for the Sublime Porte would permit, and suggested as the only means of accomplishing anything like redress that a brave impartial officer be sent to Bitlis to investigate the conduct of the governor and take the affair in his own hands. "Such a step," it was added, "might serve to save the lives of many Christians," and it was further represented that "could the assassins be brought to just sentence it would unquestionably lessen the demand for indemnity which otherwise it would be the duty of the legation to present against the Imperial Government in this connection."

On November 7, 1883, the legation of the United States, by a third note, No. 184, communicated to his highness, the minister of foreign affairs, that the governor-general of Bitlis had confronted four persons with Mr. Knapp for identification, and that that gentleman had recognized Moussa Bey as one of those who had robbed and wounded him. The legation of the United States then expressed a hope that the minister of foreign affairs would give proper orders for bringing Moussa Bey and his companions in crime before the tribunals for trial.

Still later, on November 12, 1883, the legation of the United States addressed a fourth note, No. 185, to his highness, the minister of foreign affairs, detailing again the circumstances of the attempted murder of Messrs. Knapp and Reynolds, and representing the untrustworthiness of the governor-general by charging that Moussa Bey had already obtained from him assurances of immunity in the event of a trial and conviction.

His highness, the minister, was then requested that, if it was decided to maintain the governor-general at his post, orders be given for the transfer of the criminals to Constantinople for trial.

The three notes last named of the legation of the United States have not been answered by his highness, the minister of foreign affairs, except in a note, dated December 8, 1883, in which he is pleased to renew assurances based upon telegrams from the governor-general, which are utterly unreliable.

Wherefore, abandoning hope of justice through the governor-general of Bitlis, and the judicial tribunals of the empire, the legation of the United States finds itself compelled to change its form of application for redress, and demand of the Sublime Porte indemnity in behalf of Messrs. Knapp and Reynolds, for the former £1,500, and for the latter, because of the more serious nature of his injuries, £2,000.

THE POSITION TAKEN IN WASHINGTON.

(Foreign Relations of the United States, 1884, p. 544.)

No. 419.

Mr. Frelinghuysen to Mr. Wallace.

(No. 153.)   DEPARTMENT OF STATE,
Washington, February 13, 1884.

SIR: I have to acknowledge the receipt of your No. 317, of the 25th ultimo, relative to the case of the Rev. Mr. Knapp and Dr. Reynolds, murderously attacked by Kurds near Bitlis, and to say that, after a careful consideration of all the facts before the Department, the inaction of the governor of Bitlis and the failure of the supreme Government to force him to undertake such measures as the case evidently demanded, must be regarded as a denial of justice. While this Government is always averse to making money demands for indemnity in countries whose administration of justice may differ from our own, the Department feels compelled to resort to this remedy under circumstances which manifestly make the local officers and the Government of the Porte responsible for the failure to do justice in this case.

The action reported in your dispatch is, consequently, approved.

I am, &c.,

                                        FRED'K T. FRELINGHUYSEN.

THE POSITION TAKEN IN CONSTANTINOPLE.

General Lew Wallace is understood to have been emphatically a *persona grata* as U. S. Minister to Turkey, in fact to have enjoyed, to a very exceptional degree, the personal confidence and friendship of His Majesty the present Sultan. The following quotation will show what treatment even he received in the discharge of his official duties in the case under consideration:

From the Regular Correspondent of the Tribune.

Constantinople, March 1, 1884.

The Porte, in deciding how far it is safe to affront foreign Governments, has even ranked the United States below some of the European States. The Porte during the past year has treated General Wallace as if he were the representative of a Danubian Principality. Remonstrance after remonstrance against fresh violations of the treaties it has left unanswered, and it has repeatedly omitted the courtesy of a bare acknowledgment of their receipt. In fact, Turkey has been relying upon the distance of the United States. Perhaps its officials even suppose that the American navy is afraid to risk adventures so far from home as the coasts of the Levant.

General Wallace found it necessary, for the sake of the safety of American citizens in Turkey, to press for some definition of the situation. During nearly five weeks he had been refused a personal interview with the Minister of Foreign Affairs on the ground of "indisposition." During all that time the representative of that Minister declined to enter upon any discussion of the important questions at issue. Four times the Minister Plenipotentiary of the United States had been turned away from the door of the Sublime Porte by the refusal of the Grand Vizier to see him. Each time plausible reasons were assigned which seemed to render any insistance on the part of the General uncourteous. Yet it became daily more evident that all these plausible excuses for declining negotiation on the injuries done by Turkey to American commerce and to American citizens were part of a settled purpose not to redress the wrongs.—*New York Semi-Weekly Tribune*, March 28, 1884.

THE RESULT.

The ten years that have elapsed since the above was written clearly show that what seemed then to be a " settled purpose " has become the settled policy of the Ottoman Government in regard to Americans and their rights in Turkey.

In regard to the outcome of the case of Messrs. Knapp and Raynolds, the humiliating fact must be recorded that not one cent of the indemnity demanded by the United States of America has to this day been obtained. The monster, Moussa Bey, was allowed by the Turkish Government to continue his outrages on the Armenian villages of the great Moosh plain, until his record became so appalling, that under European pressure the Porte summoned him to Constantinople, where he was entertained as the Sultan's guest. He was whitewashed by the courts, but the Sultan was prevailed upon to invite him to make a pilgrimage to Medina at his expense, and there spend the remainder of his days in religious exercises.

APPENDIX B.

U. S. CONSULATES IN EASTERN TURKEY.

The following petition was recently presented to the Hon. Walter Q. Gresham, Secretary of State, and to the Senate and House of Representatives of the United States of America, for the establishment of U. S. Consulates at Erzerum and Harpoot. The necessary legislation has been promptly enacted, for which the thanks of all Americans in Turkey is due to His Excellency the President, to the Secretary of State and to members of both Houses of Congress.

WASHINGTON, D. C., Jan. 3, 1895.

Apropos to the recent massacre of five thousand Armenians in Turkey, it is clearly inexpedient for the United States to mix up in the Eastern Question. But it is equally clear that *the duty of protecting a large body of native born American citizens constantly subjected to danger, injury and insult in that land is not complicated by any Monroe Doctrine.* In their interests, attention is called to this brief statement of facts, and to a practical request for consular protection.

1. NUMBER OF INDIVIDUALS AND INTERESTS INVOLVED.

Distributed in thirty of the principal cities of Asiatic Turkey alone, there is a permanent body of *two hundred and fifty Americans*, not including their children, who hold *over two million dollars* of American property for residence and the use of their educational, medical, publishing and religious enterprises.

These figures do not cover the large commercial interests of Americans in Turkey, for which statistics are not at hand.

2. NATURE AND EXTENT OF THE DANGER TO WHICH THEY ARE EXPOSED.

There are two sources of danger: first, the *lawlessness* of numerous highwaymen who infest the country, and of the fanatical Moslem population of the cities; and second, the *hostility* of Turkish officials, who have repeatedly failed to restrain, and in some cases have even encouraged attacks upon the lives and property of American citizens.

3. EVIDENCE OF THIS DANGEROUS CONDITION.

So far back as June 29th, 1881, Secretary Blaine, in official instructions to Minister Wallace at Constantinople, wrote:

"Your attention will doubtless be prominently and painfully drawn to the insecurity of the lives and property of foreign travelers in Turkey, and the failures of the authorities to prevent or repress outrages upon American citizens by wayside robbers and murderers, or even to execute its own laws in the rare instances of the perpetrators of such outrages being brought to justice. I cannot take a better text on which to base this instruction, than the accompanying copy of a letter addressed to the President by a number of American residents in Turkey. Its statements are known to be entirely within the truth, and can be verified abundantly from the files of your legation. They show in simple yet forcible language, the insecurity of traveling in that country, and *the instances to the number of eight, within the past two years, when American citizens have been robbed and beaten by lawless marauders.* On these occasions the lives of the assailed have been at the mercy of the robbers and, in one instance at least, the taking of life preceded the robbery."—*Foreign Relations of the United States 1881.*

The above extract refers to outrages in Western Asia Minor and the vicinity of Constantinople, but it is well known that in the Eastern and interior part of Turkey, where many of us live, *the insecurity is greater and has steadily increased, during the thirteen years that have elapsed since the above facts were admitted by the State Department.*

The murderous attack by a Kurdish chief in person, which nearly cost Dr. G. C. Raynolds, of Van his life, and for which *no indemnity was ever obtained,* though the assailant was positively identified in court, is reported in full in *Foreign Relations of the United States,* 1883, 1884, and 1890.

The arrest and indignities inflicted upon Mr. Richardson of Erzerum, by the Governor-General, for which *no apology even was ever secured,* are related in *Foreign Relations of the United States* 1891.

The burning of Marsovan College by an unrestrained Turkish mob and the *danger to the lives of many American residents* is found in *Foreign Relations of the United States* 1893.

More cases of injury and insult, may be found in the same official records. But in many other instances it has been felt to be useless and inexpedient to even report them. *The absence of any American representative to substantiate and vindicate our rights on the ground, and the hopelessness of securing anything but further injury by trying to press our claims, often drives us to the humiliating necessity of suffering injustice with scarcely a protest.*

THE REQUEST.

We feel that the condition shown by the above evidence, not to add more, abundantly justifies a renewed request for *some Consular protection in the Eastern part of Turkey, for the American citizens permanently residing there in the prosecution of lawful pursuits.* Our present exposed and helpless condition is clearly set forth in a communication from the United States Legation at Constantinople, to the State Department: " It may not be doubted that the absence of an American Consul at Erzroom leaves our citizens there singularly destitute of means to vindicate their rights and protect their interests; this is the more regrettable as Erzroom is a missionary station of considerable importance, and situated in a province where official protection is most frequently and urgently needed. *The British Consul there is instructed to act 'unofficially' for our citizens, but his right to represent them is not recognized by the Ottoman authorities; the obvious consequence is, that when his good offices are most needed, they are of least avail.*" *Foreign Relations of United States* 1891.

We are thus seen to be cut off from Consular protection of any kind. The nearest U. S. Consul, Mr. Jewett of Sivas, an excellent man, is unavailable for us for three reasons: first, the delay and difficulty in communicating with him on account of our isolation, and the very circuitous post-routes, in case the local authorities were kind enough not to intercept our letters, as they have repeatedly, even the official correspondence of the United States Minister (*Foreign Relations of the U. S.* 1893); second, the distance and methods of travel are such that probably from one to two months would elapse after any outrage, before the Sivas Consul could be notified and arrive; third, the Consul at Sivas could not leave his post without neglecting the large American interests in Asia Minor.

Aside from being needed when special difficulties do occur, it is obvious that the mere presence of a United States Consul on the ground would have a marked effect in *deterring* both the lawless and fanatical elements, and the officials, who have never seen the stars and stripes, from repeating acts which have caused much injury to the interests of American citizens, and have been *the occasion* of *tedious and unpleasant diplomatic correspondence between the two countries.* The expense of living in Turkey is unusually low.

In view of all the foregoing facts, it is urgently requested that American Consuls be located at Erzerum and Harpoot. These cities are large centres of population and of American interests, and the seat of Provincial Governors. They have large commercial and strategic importance, and as good facilities for communication by post, telegraph, or private messenger as the country affords. From Erzerum, Bitlis and Van could also be cared for, while Mardin and Mosul would naturally be under Harpoot, and thus the Americans of that whole territory would be brought within two or three week's journey of Consular protection.

We are from seven hundred to one thousand miles from Constantinople, which means a journey of three to six weeks. The fact that at least *5,000 men, women and children in our midst have been massacred, and this fact kept nearly three months from the civilized world, is a significant hint as to our isolation and danger.* The articles in the last *Harper's Weekly*, Dec. 29, and in the *Review of Reviews*, Jan. 1895, give much light on the situation.

APPENDIX C.

DR. HAMLIN'S EXPLANATION.

(New York Herald, December 20, 1894.)

To the Editor of the Herald:

A cutting from the *Herald* has been sent to me to-day containing a letter of His Excellency, Mavroyeni, on the Armenian atrocities. I must strongly object to the use he makes of a letter of mine in the Boston *Congregationalist* of last year (December 23, 1893).

The object of that letter was to show the absurdity of the revolutionary plotters. The Armenians are a noble race, but few in number, scattered and unarmed. The Turkish Government has never had the least fear of any such movement. It knows well that there is no place in the Empire where one thousand or even one hundred Armenians could assemble with hostile intent. And besides they have no arms, and they are not accustomed to their use. They would be lambs in the midst of wolves. Every one knows this who knows anything of Turkey outside of Constantinople.

It is to be greatly regretted that the Ottoman Ambassador should attempt to cover up the path of these horrid atrocities which have agitated the whole Christian world and for which Turkey must give account. It were far better to deplore the fact and work for justice and judgment. It may be the time has passed when such deeds of blood and torture, committed upon unarmed men, women and children, can be condoned by the civilized world.

The plots of the revolutionists were harmless as to any effective force, but were very pernicious in arousing fanaticism. The fact that a few hair-brained young men in foreign lands had plotted a revolution was a sufficient reason in the view of Moslem fanaticism for devoting the whole race to destruction. It was this which I feared and it is this which has happened.

Another object of the letter, from which His Excellency has quoted, was to draw attention to the fact that this revolutionary movement is a game which Russia is playing in her own interests. And she has played it well. She has again caught Turkey in her trap. The whole civilized world will now approve of her marching in with force to stop the slaughter of an industrious, peaceful, unarmed peasantry. If Russia enters, it will be with professions of great kindness toward the Sultan. It will be to aid him in his well known benevolent intentions in the government of his Christian subjects! But she will call the Armenians to her standard and will arm and train them and they will prove a brave and valiant soldiery. Some of the ablest generals of the Russian army have been Armenians. Thus armed and trained, with the aid of their Russian allies, they will defend their own homes in the Sassoun or any other district.

Turkey has brought this upon herself. His Excellency is a Greek gentleman, and has a natural sympathy with Russia. His influence has been to magnify the revolutionary plots instead of showing, as my letter did, their insignificance and their Russian character, and has led his government to give to them an importance which seems absurd. The Turkish Government has had sufficient opportunity to study and understand Russia since the Treaty of 1829, and again of 1833. Have her trusted advisers been true to her, or have they betrayed her interests?

The civilized and Christian world awaits with profound and fixed attention the solution of the question whether bloody, fanatical violence or law shall reign over the Eastern regions of the Turkish Empire.

CYRUS HAMLIN.

Lexington, Mass., December 18, 1894.

APPENDIX D.

THE CENSORSHIP OF THE PRESS.

With what intelligence and religious toleration the censorship of the press is conducted may be judged from examples found in an official document:

"The quotation, in religious books, of the words of Scripture for proof or illustration, has been subjected to the will of the censor; and even the printing of religious books has been objected to on the ground that since Christians are graciously allowed to use the Holy Bible, they need no other books of religion. Appeal from the decisions of the censors is practically unavailing. This censor insists that the Scriptural phrase 'Kingdom of Christ' may not be used by Christians. . . .

"The index list of the Bible lessons for 1893 is simply a table of contents prepared by the British Sunday School Union. The censors have refused to permit the publication of this index list, unless some fifty titles are erased, or modified into a form at variance with the matter of the lessons, or expanded to a degree impossible in a brief table of contents, for example: St. Luke iv., 14-21, 'Gospel liberty.' The word 'liberty' must be erased. Jeremiah xxxiii., 7-16, 'Sorrow turned to joy.' This title must be suppressed. Haggai ii., 1-9, 'Encouraging the people.' This title, which refers to the Divine encouragement given to the people in the work of rebuilding the temple in the days of Zerubbabel, must be erased.

"Psalm xxxiii., 10-22, 'Wicked devices frustrated.' This title must be stricken out.

"Esther iv., 1-9, 'Sorrow in the palace.' This title must be suppressed.

"Romans iv., 1-8, 'Saved by grace.' This title must be modified to read 'Saved from sin by grace.'

"Psalm xxxviii., 8-15, 'Hope in distress.' This title must be suppressed.

"Joshua i., 1-9, 'Fear not.' This title can not be allowed.

"Romans viii., 31-39, 'Rejoicing in persecution.' This title must be erased.

"Romans xv., 25-33, 'A benevolent object.' This title cannot be allowed to stand unless the object is stated."—*Foreign Relations of the United States*, 1893.

We learn that four months after the complaint was made the particular points specified above were arranged. But as soon as foreign pressure was relaxed the activity of the Censor revived, and is now more intolerable than ever. A gentleman of long experience and intimate knowledge writing from behind the scenes within a month, states: "The Censorship of the Press is so severe as to amount almost to a prohibition. At Constantinople a most reckless and destructive mutilation of books goes on; and, contrary to the expressed utterances of the Porte guaranteeing religious liberty, Christian doctrines are expunged or changed, so as, at times, to become ridiculous and false. The men appointed as Censors of the Press seem to be utterly ignorant of all Christian literature and history and their object is to make all books conform to the doctrines of Islam.

"The religious weekly of the American Mission in Syria, which had been published for thirty years, was suppressed for a whole year, no reason being given; and when the permit was finally secured, it was accompanied by puerile and humiliating conditions."

Some special departments of literature, such as history and poetry, are forbidden, wholesale, by the Censor. Many of the Censor's decisions and the grounds on which they are based would be most laughable, but for the fact that they are part of an attempt to throttle and starve the hungry and growing minds of millions.

APPENDIX E.

PARTIAL BIBLIOGRAPHY OF THE SUBJECT.

HISTORICAL.

NORMAN, *Armenia and the Campaign of 1877.* London, 1878.

MILNER, *The Turkish Empire.* London: Religious Tract Society.

CLARK, *The Arabs and the Turks.* New York: Dodd & Mead.

TOZER, *The Church and the Eastern Empire.* New York: Randolph. London: Longmans.

LATIMER, *Russia and Turkey in the XIX. Century.* Chicago: McClurg & Co., 1894.

MORFILL, *Russia.* New York: Putnams. London: T. Fisher Unwin, 1893.

LANE POOLE, *Turkey.* New York: Putnams. London: T. Fisher Unwin, 1893.

CHURCHILL, *Druzes and Maronites.* London: Quaritch, 1862.

Viscount STRATFORD DE REDCLIFFE, *The Eastern Question.* London: John Murray, 1881.

LATHAM, *Russian and Turk.* London: Allen, 1878.

LAYARD, *Nineveh and its Remains.* London: Murray.

RAWLINSON, *The Five Great Monarchies.* Murray.

RAWLINSON, *The Sixth Great Oriental Monarchy.* Longmans.

RAWLINSON, *The Seventh Great Oriental Monarchy.* Longmans.

TRAVEL.

SMITH and DWIGHT, *Researches in Armenia.* 2 vols. Boston: Crocker & Brewster, 1833.

STEPHENS, *Greece, Turkey, Russia, and Poland.* 2 vols. New York: Harpers, 1839.

SOUTHGATE, *A Tour through Armenia, Persia, and Mesopotamia.* 2 vols. New York: D. Appleton & Co., 1840.

VAN LENNEP, *Travels in Asia Minor.* 2 vols. New York: Van Lennep, 1870.

VAN LENNEP, *Bible Lands: Their Modern Customs and Manners.* New York: Harpers, 1875.

THIELMANN, *Journey in the Caucasus, Persia, and Turkey.* 2 vols. London: 1875.

CREAGH, *Armenians, Koords, and Turks.* London: 1880.

TOZER, *Turkish Armenia and Eastern Asia Minor.* London: 1881.

BISHOP, *Journeys in Persia and Kurdistan.* 2 vols. New York: Putnams. London: John Murray, 1891.

MOHAMMEDANISM.

SALE'S, *The Koran.* 2 vols. Philadelphia: Wardle, 1833.

SMITH, R. Bosworth, *Mohammed and Mohammedanism.* London: John Murray. New York: Harpers, 1875.

WASHBURN, *The Points of Contact and Contrast between Christianity and Mohammedanism.* Chicago: The Parliament Publishing Company, 1893.

BURTON, *Pilgrimage to El Medinah and Mecca.* New York: Putnams. Belfast: Mullan.

MUIR, *Life of Mahomet.* London.

SPRENGER, *Life of Mohammed.* Allahabad, 1851.

IRVING, *Life of Mahomet.* Putnams.

STOBART, *Islam and its Founder.* Christian Knowledge Soc.

PFANDER, *Mezan el Hoc.* London: Church Missionary Society.

HUGHES, *Notes on Muhammadanism.* London: Allen, 1877.

OSBORN, *Islam under the Arabs.* London: Longmans, Green.

MUIR, *The Coran.* London: Christian Knowledge Society.

KOELLE, *Mohammed and Mohammedanism.* London: Rivington's, 1889.

ARNOLD, *Islam and Christianity.* London: Longmans.

AMEER ALI, *The Spirit of Islam.*

AMEER ALI, *Life and Teachings of Mohammed.* London: Williams.

Appendix.

MISSIONS.

The Missionary Herald, 1820-1894. Boston: The American Board.

DWIGHT, *Christianity Revived in the East*. New York: Baker & Scribner, 1850.

ANDERSON, *Missions to the Oriental Churches*. 2 vols. Boston: Congregational Publishing Society, 1872.

WHEELER, *Letters from Eden*. Boston: American Tract Society, 1868.

WHEELER, *Ten Years on the Euphrates*. Boston: American Tract Society, 1860.

WHEELER, *Daughters of Armenia*. New York: American Board, 1891.

PRIME, *Forty Years in the Turkish Empire*, or Memoirs of Rev. William Goodell, D.D., Boston: American Tract Society, 1877.

LAURIE, *Missions and Science*. Boston: American Board, 1885.

LAURIE, *Dr. Grant and the Mountain Nestorians*. Boston: Gould & Lincoln, 1853.

JESSUP, *The Mohammedan Missionary Problem*. Philadelphia: Presbyterian Board of Publication, 1879.

SCHAUFFLER, *Autobiography*. New York: Randolph, 1888.

HAMLIN, *Among the Turks*. New York: Robt. Carter & Bro.

HAMLIN, *My Life and Times*. Boston: Congregational S. S. and Pub. Soc.

ARMENIAN HISTORY.

MOSES CHORENENSIS, *Armenian History*, Arm. and Lat. London: William and George Whiston, 1736.

LANGLOIS, VICTOR, *Collection des Historiens anciens et modernes de l'Arménie*, en Français. Vol. i. Historiens grecs et syriens traduits anciennement en Arménien. Vol. II. Historiens arméniens de 5ᵉ siècle. 8º. Paris, 1867.

DULAURIER, *Recueil des Historiens des Croisades. Documents Arméniens*. Paris, 1869. Folio with fac-simile reproductions. Pp. 855. Arm. and French.

DULAURIER, *Étude sur l'Organisation Politique, Religieuse et Administrative du Royaume de la Petite-Arménie à l'époque des Croisades*. Paris, 1862.

LENORMANT, *Sur l'Ethnographie et l'Histoire de l'Arménie, avant les Achéménides*. In Lettres Assyriologiques. 1871.

Inscriptions d'un Reliquaire Arménien. With plates. Paris, 1883.

NEUMANN, *The History of Vartan by Elisaeus.* Translated from the Armenian. London, 1830.

MALAN, *The Life and Times of St. Gregory the Illuminator.* Translated from Armenian. London, 1868.

Chamich, *History of Armenia.* Translated from Armenian into English by Avdall. Calcutta, 1827.

STUBBS, WILLIAM. *The Mediæval Kingdoms of Cyprus and Armenia.* In Seventeen Lectures, etc. 1886.

Genealogical Catalogue of the Kings of Armenia. Oriental Translation Fund. Vol. ii. London, 1834.

GABRIELIAN, *The Armenians or People of Ararat.* Philadelphia: Allen, Lane & Scott, 1892.

ARMENIAN LITERATURE.

NÈVE, FÉLIX, *L'Arménie Chrétienne et sa Littérature.* Louvain, 1886.

Catalogue des anciennes traductions Arméniennes, siècles iv.–xiii. 8vo pp. 783. Venezia, 1889.

DWIGHT, *Catalogue of all Works known to exist in the Armenian Language earlier than the Seventeenth Century.* American Oriental Society. Vol. iii. 1853.

FORTESCUE, *The Armenian Church, History, Literature, Doctrine.* London, 1872.

ISSAVERDENZ, *The Divine Ordinances according to the Catholic Armenian Ritual.* Venice, 1867.

ALISHAN, *Armenian Popular Songs.* Armenian and English. Venice, 1867.

LORD BYRON'S *Armenian Exercises and Poetry.* Armenian and English. Venice, 1870.

GENERAL INDEX.

A

ABERDEEN, Lord, 72
AGHTAMAR, 141, 145
ALEXANDER, 53, 133
AMERICANS
    Position, 67, 148
    Number, 149
    Work, 141, 148-151
    Influence, 152-154
    Interests, 147-166
ANGLO-ARMENIAN ASSOC., 69
ANGLO-TURKISH CONVENTION
  See England
ARMENIA
  Land
    Name, 44, 46
    Extent, 45
    Aspects, 44-46
    Inhabitants, 45, 46
    Condition, 9, 15, 32, 35, 39, 42, 46, 62-65
    Autonomy, 69, 81
  Race
    Origin, 132
    Number, 45, 142
    Distribution, 44
    Characteristics, 52, 140
    Condition, chap. i., ii., iii., iv.

" Revolution," Preface, Chap. i., 69, 81, 167
Progress, 79, 117, 154
History
  Biblical, 132, 133
  Classical, 134, 135
  Armenian Sources, 144
  In General, 53
Church
  Apostolic Tradition, 136
  Founder, 136
  Doctrine, 137
  Form, 137, 144
  Heroic Struggle, 53
  Decline, 139
  Reform, 140, 143, 154
  Catholicos, 137, 138
  Political Significance, 138
  Future, 138
Literature
  Language, 132, 143
  Pre-Christian, 143
  Golden Age, 144
  Second Period, 144
  Modern Revival, 146
  General Character, 144
Massacre
  See Massacres
ARNAUT, 98

General Index.

AUSTRIA, Preface, 104
AUTHOR, Purpose, Preface, 147

B

BAGDAD, 48
BAIBOURT, 46
BASHI-BAZOUK, 98, 102
BASHKALLA, 16, 49
BERLIN TREATY. See Treaties
BIBLIOGRAPHY, Appendix E
BILOTTI, Consul, 113
BISHOP, Mrs., 62, 67, 131, 154
BISMARCK, Preface, 78
BITLIS, 12, 16, 37, 43
BLUE-BOOKS. See England
BLOWITZ, M. de, 83
BOSNIA, 83, 84
BRITANNICA, Encyc., 48, 49
BRYCE, Hon. James, Preface, 69
BULGARIA, 73, 83, 96, 101, 126
BYRON, Lord, 154
BYZANTINE EMPIRE, 53, 134

C

CAIRO UNIVERSITY, 75
CASTLE, Kurdish, 49
CATHOLICOS. See Armenia
CENSORSHIP, 73, Append. C
CHERMSIDE, Consul, 113
CHIOS, 97
CHOSROES, 137
CHRISTIANITY, Toleration. See Mohammedanism
CHURCHILL, 96, 100
CIRCASSIANS, 73
CODE NAPOLEON, 89
COMMISSION of Inquiry. See Massacres

CONSULAR Reports.
    British. See England
    United States, 66
COUNCIL of Chalcedon, 157
COURTS. See Turkey
CRETE. See Massacres
CRIMEAN War, 72
CRISIS, 33, 35, 82, 84, Preface
CYPRUS Convention, 72, 76

D

DIARBEKIR, 48
DIPLOMACY
    American, Preface, Append. A, B
    European, Preface, Chap. v.
    Turkish, 70, 77, 93

E

EASTERN QUESTION, Preface, 68, 85
EDUCATION, 87, 140, 143, 150, 155
EGYPT, 83
ENGLAND
    Attitude, Preface
    Responsibility, 69, 73, 76, 79, 103, 128. See Treaties
    Efforts, 76-79, 123
    Consular Reports, Preface, 48, 66, 68, 74, 77, 78, 112
ERZERUM, 46, 62, 66, 113
ERZINGAN, 21, 23, 46
EVERETT, Consul, 113

F

FANATICISM. See Mohammedanism

General Index.

FRANCE, Preface, 78, 104, 107, 138, 140, 149
FREEMAN, 79, 85, 88, 117

G

GENGHIS KHAN, 130
GERMANY, Preface, 78, 104
GLADSTONE, on
    Consular Reports, Preface
    Sassoun Massacre, 121-125
    Turkish Rule, 126-130
GOSCHEN, 78
GRANVILLE, 77
GREECE, 83, 89, 97, 127, 133, 154
GREGORY, The Illuminator. See Armenian Church

H

HALLWARD, Consul, 16
HAMLIN, Cyrus, 81, 167
HANNIBAL, 134
HARPOOT, 48
HATTI HUMAYOUN, 72
HATTI SHERIF, 71
HERODOTUS, 133
HERZEGOVINA, 183
HUGHES, 89
HUMANITY, Preface, 1, 33, 123, 127, 129

I

IBRAHIM PASHA, 71
IDENTICAL NOTE, 76
"ILLUMINATOR," 53, 137, 138. See Armenian Church
IMPERIAL RESCRIPT, 71

INDEPENDENT, The, 54, 95, 101
INFORMATION
    Channels, 66
    Danger of, Preface, 1, 15, 16, 54, 62
    Sultan's, 13, 89, 92, 93
ISLAM. See Mohammedanism
ITALY, Preface, 104

J

JACOBITE, 54, 89
JESSUP, 75
JESUIT, 137
JEWS, 68, 89

K

KALLAY, M. de, 84
KERMANSHAH, 46
KHRIMIAN, Catholicos, 138
    Motto on Title-page
KHOSHAB, Castle, 50
KNAPP, Attack on, 157
KORAN. See Mohammedanism
KURDISTAN
    Country, 46
    Kurds, 48-52
    "Hamidieh" Troops, 1-30, 126
    Outrages, 54-69, 157-164

L

LATHAM, 96
LAYARD, 96, 99
LEBANON, 93
LEON VI., 136
LLOYD, Consul-Gen., 66

M

MacCall, Canon, 72
MacGahan, 96, 103
Malatiah, 46
Mamelukes, 136
Maronites, 99
Massacres in Turkey
   Greek (1822), 96–98
   Nestorian (1850), 96, 99
   Syrian (1860), 96, 99
   Cretan (1867), 104
   Bulgarian (1876), 96, 101
   Armenian (1877), 105–107
   Yezidi (1892), 108
   Armenian (1894), Chap. I.
     Victims, Dedication
     Evidence, 1–42
     Uncalled for, 21, 23, 26, 36
     Premeditated, 17, 18
     Ordered, 7, 12, 14, 20, 28–30
     Long Duration, 21, 31
     Number Slain, 11, 15, 24
     Manner, 20–23, 26, 31
     Violation of Women, 15, 22, 27, 28, 39, 41
     Denials, 12, 25, 27
     Concealment, 11–15, 29–34, 40
     Commission of Inquiry, Preface, 103
     Gladstone's Opinion, 121–125
Midhat Pasha, 86
Missions. See Americans
   Other Missions, 149
Mohammedanism
   Founder, 110, 125
   Koran, 89, 99, 111, 115
   Exclusive, 115, 116
   Spirit, 22, 74, 89, 110, 167
   Rationalistic Types, 116
   "Tolerance," 42, 71, 74, 84, 107, 114, 127, 169
   Converts from, 68, 114
   Union with State, 111, 119
Moosh, 43
Morfill, 69
Mosul, 48, 58

N

Nebuchadnezzar, 53
Nestorians, 54, 89. See Massacres
Norman, 52, 85, 104

O

Ordos, 70
Ottoman. See Turkey

P

Pagratide, 134
Parry, 107
Parthians, 53, 134
Persia, 6, 43, 48, 53
Phil-Armenic, 69
Pope, 88
Porte Sublime
   See Sultan of Turkey
Powers, European
   Attitude, Preface, 67, 76, 81, 99, 104
   Responsibility, 33, 41, 69, 88, 119, 122
Protestants
   Origin, 153
   Number, 150
   Success, 147–154
   Hostility to, 58, 71, 155

R

RAYNOLDS, Attack on, 157, 163
REGISTER, The Christian, 127
RELIGION
    Classification by, 152
        Freedom of, 70–75, 110–120, 169
        See Mohammedanism, Turkey
REVIEW OF REVIEWS, Preface
ROBERT COLLEGE, 115, 149, 155
ROLIN-JAEQUEMYNS, 78, 112
ROMANS, 53
RUPENIAN Dynasty, 136, 144
RUSSIA
    Attitude, 53, 68, 104, 168
    Feeling toward, 45, 52, 68, 73, 81

S

SALADIN, 48
SARACEN, 53
SASSANIDÆ, 134
SCHUYLER, EUGENE, 96, 101
SELJUK, 53, 136
SELEUCIDÆ, 133
SHAH, 48
SHAW, DR. ALBERT, 7
SIOUFFI, 107
SMITH, R. Bosworth, 111
STAMBOUL, 70
STEIN, ROBERT, 96
STEVENSON, Preface, 121
STILLMAN, 104
STRATFORD DE REDCLIFFE, Lord, 69, 109
STRONG, DR. JOSIAH, Introduction

SUBLIME PORTE, 90–94, 155
SULTAN
    Mohammed II, 87, 152
    Selim I., 88
    Mahmoud, 97
    Medjid, 71, 72
    Abd-ul-Hamid, Preface
        Sincerity, 13, 87, 91, 155
        Helplessness, 88
        Isolation, 124
        Absolutism, 90–94
SYRIAN, 89, 96, 100
    See Massacres

T

TACITUS, 134
TAMERLANE, 136
TIGRANES II., 134
TIMES, THE LONDON, 104, 127
TOZER, 136
TREATIES, Chapter iv.
    Adrianople, 70
    Berlin, 69, 73, 76–81, 112
    Cyprus, Preface, 73, 76
    Paris, 72
TREBIZOND, 12, 43, 113
TURKEY
    Americans in. See Americans, United States
    Antecedents, 117–120, 124, 127
    Attitude, Preface, 81
    Future, 108–109, 120, 127–130
    Government
        Administration, 11, 35, 46, 74, 109, 123, 128, 153
        Courts, 41, 65, 74, 112
        Divided, 92

www.ingramcontent.com/pod-product-compliance
Lightning Source LLC
Chambersburg PA
CBHW021729220426
43662CB00008B/773